Accademia
Galleries
of Venice

Giovanna Nepi Sciré
Francesco Valcanover

Accademia Galleries of Venice

Electa

Translation from Italian
Michael Ph. Langley
Paul Blanchard

Printed in Italy
© 1985 by Edizioni Electa SpA - Milano

Preface

The Accademia Galleries, the largest museum structure of Venice and the Veneto region, offer an unparalleled survey of five centuries of Venetian painting. After the Accademia was moved, in 1807, from the Fonteghetto della Farina to the Gothic Scuola and Church of Santa Maria della Carità and Palladio's Convento dei Canonici Lateranensi (which in themselves represent a monumental complex of great historic and artistic interest), the collections grew steadily; so much so that as soon as the Galleries became independent, in the late nineteenth century, the works exhibited were restricted to panels and canvases of the Venetian School. The remaining material, including non-Venetian paintings, were distributed among other institutes.

Thus, today, the visitor to the Accademia Galleries may trace the development of Venetian art from the fourteenth to the eighteenth century through its most outstanding examples, from the first historical figures, Paolo Veneziano and Lorenzo, to the exponents of the International Gothic style; from the pioneers of the Early Renaissance, Gentile and Giovanni Bellini, Vittore Carpaccio and Giambattista Cima da Conegliano, to the modernizers of Western painting, Giorgione and Tiziano, and the great figures of the late sixteenth century, Jacopo Tintoretto, Paolo Veronese and Jacopo Bassano; from the voices of the Seicento, certainly less important in the context of European painting in that century, but nevertheless original and independent, to the outstanding personalities of the Settecento, who produced a kaleidoscopic variety of refined and poetic "genres" which won them recognition throughout Europe.

Even a brief glance at the Accademia collections reveals how Venetian painting, as soon as it had achieved independent originality, maintained for five centuries an unfailing fidelity to the clear, conscious choice of two basic expressive values: color and light. This same choice is reflected with perfect coherence in all other art forms, and even in the appearance of the city itself, "built in a form that is not classical, but open and unaffected by time" (S. Bettini). Given the important role that the Accademia Galleries play in furthering the knowledge and understanding of one of the greatest artistic cultures of all times, the attentive visitor immediately notices the handicaps under which the institute is compelled to work as a result of the desperate lack of space. Undoubtedly, many things have been done to enliven and modernize the Galleries since the end of the Second World War. These include the more rational arrangement of the collections; the creation of new, easy to visit warehouses; the establishment of a Restoration Laboratory and a space for temporary exhibitions; the introduction of year-round temperature and humidity controls in the Drawing Cabinet; the installation of fire sensors and antitheft devices; and the upgrading of many other services.

But the acquisition of new space is the only means for reaching the more fundamental objectives of an animated and productive institute of advanced conception. Most importantly, the collections could be arranged in such a way as to present the essential development of Venetian painting without distracting interruptions and backtracking; and an area could be set up where visitors would be welcomed with ease and introduced to the history of the buildings and the collection, and where the acquisition of high quality books and photographs of Venetian art would be facilitated. Furthermore, only through the availability of new spaces can certain pre-existent services be restructured and partially "reinvented". The Drawing Cabinet is in need of a room for consultation and another for temporary exhibitions of material from the extensive stores of prints and drawings; the warehouses must become genuine galleries in their own right, open to all; the teaching activity, today confined to an austere "all-purpose" room, must be extended as more rooms become available; and the interior of the former Church of the Carità should be restored to its original form and devoted entirely to temporary exhibitions. The Restoration Laboratory must be enlarged to include at least five rooms for the restoration of wood, canvas, and paper. Nor, finally, should rest and refreshment areas be neglected.

This expansion of the Accademia Galleries, in the context of a serious and concrete city-wide cultural policy, could easily be achieved in the short run by moving the Academy proper to classrooms better suited to modern teaching standards, say, in a part of the Arsenal — the utilization of which has been, and continues to be, a matter of debate. In this way the "great" Accademia Galleries would take on their proper role as a major European museum, and the Academy itself would receive

6　a fresh charge of vital energy.

The two institutions would no longer be constrained, by lack of space and financial resources, to a mortifying existence of limited cultural and social significance. In the meantime, as Venice and Italy continue to evolve, the Accademia Galleries and the other museums of the city, burdened with difficulties arising from a nearsighted consciousness of their true importance, will continue to act as unique catalysts for the knowledge of Venetian art.

Francesco Valcanover
Soprintendente ai Beni Artistici e Storici di Venezia

Introduction

The Accademia Galleries of Venice[1], like the Brera Pinacoteca or the Accademia of Bologna, occupy a unique place in the history of early nineteenth-century Italy. They are "political" museums whose origin is closely related to local events of historical importance. For Venice this means the decline of the city to the status of a mere pawn of the Great Powers of Europe.

With the annexation of Venice to the Kingdom of Italy following the Presburg Treaty of December 26, 1805, and with the decrees that followed in 1806, 1808, and 1810, all public palaces, 40 parishes, and 176 religious buildings were closed. Still others were demolished. The works of art that came from these buildings and that were not sold off or lost, were brought to the Accademia for safekeeping.

Originally, the aim of this massive transfer of artworks, which took place throughout the kingdom, was educational. This much is clear from the decree of September 1, 1803 (extended to Venice on February 12, 1807), which called for the establishment of pluridisciplinary art schools together with picture galleries for "the use of those who practice the profession of painting".

The Venetian Academy was also ordered to move from the Fonteghetto della Farina to that complex of buildings, also acquired following the suppressions, which includes the Convento dei Canonici Lateranensi, designed in 1561 by Andrea Palladio, the Church of the Carità, rebuilt by Bartolomeo Bon between 1441 and 1452, and the Scuola della Carità, the first of the great Venetian Schools, founded in 1260. Thus there arose the parallel problem of relocating the new institution in spaces originally designed for a very different purpose, and housed in different buildings which obviously were not connected with one another. The faculty immediately voiced its perplexity concerning the new location of the Academy, at a considerable distance from the center of the city and on the far bank of the canal, over which the present bridge had not yet been built. (The situation is described in a painting by Canaletto in the National Gallery in London, which also shows the bell-tower, now collapsed.) The faculty also objected to the limited number of rooms available without tampering with Palladio's building, and to the enormous expenditures that this would entail. But the government stood by its decision and the Academy, which had hoped to be relocated in the neighborhood of Santi Giovanni and Paolo, was instead itself obliged to set up shop in quarters it had acknowledged as very poorly suited indeed to its purposes.

The restructuring of the new buildings, completed in 1810 by Giannantonio Selva, devastated the church, which, deprived of its altars and furnishings, was divided horizontally and vertically to make five large rooms on the ground floor for the Scuola and two exhibition halls on the floor above, conceived, after the Gothic windows had been walled up, with overhead lighting. The problem of connecting the two buildings on the first floor was solved by opening up a passageway in the end wall of the Sala dell'Albergo and building a small staircase which gave access to the halls through a vestibule.

The rooms of the Scuola were largely unaltered. The late fifteenth-century wooden ceiling of the Sala dell'Albergo (Room XXIV) has been preserved, as have the triptych by Antonio Vivarini and Giovanni d'Alemagna dated 1446 and the *Presentation* executed by Tiziano between August 31, 1534 and March 6, 1539. The other paintings comprising this cycle, the *Marriage of the Virgin* by Giampietro Silvio and the *Annunciation* by Girolamo Dente, are today in the Parrocchiale di Mason Vicentino. Almost intact, except for the removal of the altar, is the large Chapter Room (Room I), where the magnificent blue and gold coffered ceiling carved by Marco Cozzi between 1461 and 1484, and completely covered with pure gold in 1756, may still be seen. The five central high-reliefs were removed around 1814 and replaced with four *Prophets* by Domenico Campagnola, removed from the Scuola della Madonna del Parto in Padua, and a *God the Father*, traditionally attributed to Alvise Vivarini but more probably by Pier Maria Pennacchi, formerly in the Oratory of San Girolamo in Venice.

The task of adapting the Convent proved more arduous, in spite of the fact that Palladio's original building had already been damaged by a fire in 1630. Selva respected the existing design in its essence, but walled up the arcades of the Ionic loggia as far as the springing of the arches, to create more wall space for hanging works in the interior. The windows facing the Rio di Sant'Agnese were raised and the top-floor cells were remodelled to obtain the School of Engraving and faculty housing.

The Pinacoteca was opened on August 10, 1817 to the general public as well as to specialists, and visitors came in droves. The appearance of the first room, where Tiziano's Frari *Assumption of*

*Giuseppe Borsato, Commemoration of Canova
in the Meeting Hall of the Scuola Grande della
Carità.*

8   *the Virgin*, acquired in 1816 by President Leopoldo Cicognara, hung next to sixteenth-century paintings of the Venetian School, is documented with almost photographic precision in a painting by Giuseppe Borsato executed in 1822 during the commemoration of Canova.
The prime constituents of the early collections were few in number, and represented mainly gifts and samples by Academy members brought over from the old building; a few paintings from the Scuola della Carità that had remained on site; and Abbot Farsetti's collection of plaster casts, acquired by the Austrian government in 1805. The first curator was Pietro Edwards, who had served as keeper of public paintings from 1778 to the fall of the Republic. All the governments that ruled Venice considered Edwards an able and conscientious public servant. After assisting the French commissioners in their choice of the works to present to Napoleon in 1797, he covered similar positions under the Austrians and under the Kingdom of Italy, becoming the latter's "curator of state

depositories". The overlapping of competencies that sometimes ran counter to the interests of the Galleries placed him in an ambiguous position and left him powerless to impede the exodus of major paintings toward Milan, or the dismantling of important complexes. And although later on Academy Secretary Antonio Diedo was allowed to select works for the Galleries from the state depositories, in exchange he was compelled to send Venetian masterpieces to Brera, and it was only through the desperate prayers of the Venetians that Tiziano's *Saint John the Baptist* in the Church of Santa Maria Maggiore was allowed to remain in the city. Fortunately it was soon joined by other paintings brought back from France, such as Paolo Veronese's *Supper in the House of Levi*, works removed for safekeeping from Venetian churches like that of San Giobbe, or donations by the Academy's first private patrons.
Important groups of works came to the Galleries as bequests. The Gerolamo Molin bequest in 1816 contained an interesting group of primitives, in-

cluding the School of Rimini *Passion Stories*, triptychs by Alberegno and Jacobello del Fiore, Lorenzo Veneziano's polyptych with the *Annunciation*, and Giambono's *Paradise*. Canova's brother donated two large plaster casts, representing *Theseus* and *Hercules*. The Felicita Renier bequest came to the museum in 1833 (but became executory only in 1850): it included such works as Piero della Francesca's *St. Jerome*, Giovanni Bellini's *Madonna and Two Saints* and *Madonna with Saints Catherine and Mary Magdalene*, and Cima's *Deposed Christ*. Lastly, in 1838 Girolamo Contarini donated his vast collection of 188 paintings, among them the *Madonna of the small trees* showing the Madonna and Child giving his blessing, Giovanni Bellini's *Allegories*, Cima's *Madonna and two Saints*, Boccaccino's *Marriage of St. Catherine*, *Sacred Conversation* attributed to Sebastiano del Piombo, and six Venetian views by Pietro Longhi.

A few important acquisitions, hand-picked on a market brimming with masterpieces, increased the Galleries' holdings even further. Yet the collection continued to be considered — and is still considered today — solely as an anthology of Venetian painting, ill-suited to a comprehensive art education. The efforts made throughout the nineteenth century to remedy this situation were unsuccessful, and when interest in the collection's educational value waned at the end of the century, this aspect was forgotten.

Nevertheless, in 1822 the Accademia managed to anticipate Brera in the acquisition, through Abbot Celotti, of the prestigious Giuseppe Bossi Collection of drawings. The collection counted more than 3000 pieces. In addition to drawings by Leonardo da Vinci and his circle, it included works by Bolognese, Roman, Tuscan, Ligurian, and Lombard masters, and by German, French, and Flemish artists. Two years later, Celotti's mediation brought the Galleries another corpus of 602 drawings from the Giacomo Quarenghi Collection.

The more works arrived, the more cramped and overcrowded the Galleries became. This would prove to be a permanent problem. Selva drew up a plan for expansion, but died before he could carry it out (1819). The plan was taken up by his successor, Francesco Lazzari, who built the two large rooms on the left of Palladio's Convent (Rooms XI and X). Both rooms were finished in 1828 and the first was opened to the public (the second opened six years later, in 1834). Four columns of Greek marble were brought from the Scuola della Misericordia to adorn the doorway between the two rooms.

Lazzari went on to rework the Convent in 1829. He destroyed the arches of Palladio's courtyard, which Selva had left intact, and he added two more bays. He also tore down the walls blocking the Ionic colonnade which, like the Doric colonnade, would later be enclosed in glass.

In 1830 further modifications were carried out on the façade. The Carità's emblems were replaced by those of the Academy, niches were pierced to make windows, and the wall was crowned by Antonio Giacarelli's statue of *Minerva riding the Adriatic Lion*, now in the Giardini Pubblici.

At this time the large ground-floor room that appears in the Combatti plan of 1847 was subdivided to give the Galleries an entrance independent of the School, while the lunettes in the ceiling of Room I were decorated with portraits of major Venetian artists, executed by painters and students of the Academy. Finally, between 1849 and 1856 the complete intercommunication of all the rooms was achieved by the construction of the wing containing the "new rooms" (the present Rooms VI, VII, VIII and IX).

During this period the collections continued to grow, mainly as a result of Austrian Emperor Francis Joseph's acquisition in 1856 of important paintings from the Galleria Manfrin, including Nicolò di Pietro's *Madonna*, Mantegna's *St. George*, Memling's *Portrait of a Young Man*, Giovanni Agostino da Lodi's *Washing of the Feet*, and Giorgione's *Old Woman*.

This state of affairs changed little in the years immediately following the annexation of Venice to the Kingdom of Italy. After 1870, however, the collections and the School began to go their separate ways, and this separation received official sanction in the decrees of 1878 and 1879. The President of the Academy, initially appointed to "oversee" the collections, was given full curatorial powers by the School in 1881. On March 13 of the following year the collections were made completely independent both of the School and of the Academy.

A comprehensive rearrangement of the Pinacoteca, where in the meantime a new room had been built to plans by Giacomo Franco to house the *Assumption* (Room II, 1886), was begun in 1895 by curator Giulio Cantalamessa. By eliminating the nineteenth-century artists and grouping the few paintings of the other Italian and

Francesco Lazzari, Plan for the installation of
Tiziano's Assumption in Room I and of
Canova's Hercules and Lyca.

Francesco Lazzari, Section of a room.

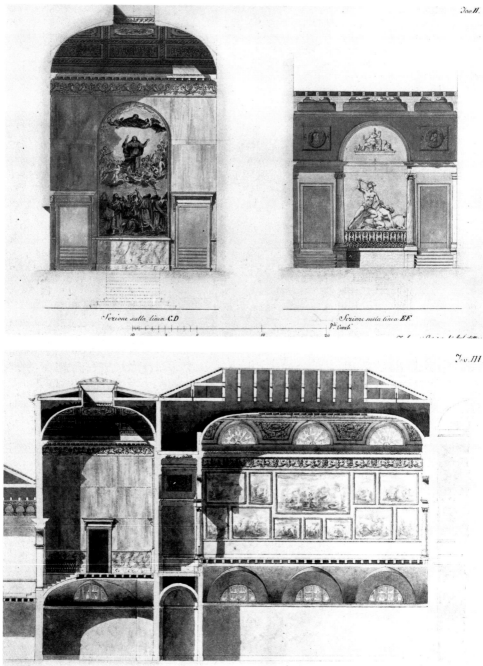

The Church of the Carità as arranged by Gino Fogolari, in the years following the First World War.

foreign schools together, he attempted the first chronological arrangement of the collections. The fifteenth-century decorative cycles from the Scuola di San Giovanni Evangelista and the Scuola di Sant'Orsola, which had not been visible as a whole previously, were reassembled in two rooms of the church. The *Stories of St. Ursula* were even arranged in an expressly planned octagonal space with overhead lighting which, although it did not claim to correspond to the original site of the piece (of which one had only a vague idea), assured the continuity of the pictorial narrative. The other rooms were hung with Venetian paintings of the sixteenth century. Cantalamessa also put Tiziano's *Presentation* back in the dimly lighted Sala dell'Albergo, from which it had been removed in 1828; for like a certain segment of his public, he rightly believed that the work should be seen in the same kind of light it had been painted for. He went on to replace the eighteenth-century benches with the present sixteenth-century dossals. Finally he eliminated the bronzes (the plaster casts had already been loaned to the School as teaching aids), which were later reunited in the Galleria Franchetti at Ca' d'Oro. Under Cantalamessa's curatorship the Galleries became more and more a showplace of Venetian art of the fourteenth to seventeenth century. Cantalamessa was also fond of making new acquisitions; he added to the collections such works as Crivelli's *Sts. Peter and Paul*, Cosmè Tura, Basaiti's *St. George*, Palma the Elder's *Sacred Conversation*, Lorenzo Veneziano's *Mystic Marriage of St. Catherine*, Paolo Veronese's *Hercules and Ceres*, and two early paintings by Tiepolo.

Cantalamessa was succeeded in 1905 by Gino Fogolari, who respected the existing arrangement of the Galleries and concentrated his energies on the acquisition of new paintings and drawings. During his long term as curator, the Galleries acquired two more paintings by Tiepolo, the companion pieces of the others; Pennacchi's *Death of the Virgin*; Bellini's organ panels from the Church of the Miracoli; Romanino's *Deposition*; Luca Giordano's *Crucifixion of St. Peter*; Strozzi's *Supper*; the portrait of Fra Galgario; Paolo Veneziano's *Madonna*; Tiepolo's bozzetto for the *Exaltation of the Cross*; and lastly, in 1932,

12 Giorgione's *Storm*. After the First World War he made every effort to assure that the works of art taken from Venice by the Austrians were returned. During the war the more important works had been removed to Florence for safekeeping. When they were returned, between 1921 and 1923, the museum was given a completely new order. The most clamorous event was the restitution of the *Assumption* to the Church of the Frari; the room designed for the immense panel immediately appeared as it appears today, disproportionately large. The areas of the church occupied by the *Stories of St. Ursula* and the *Miracles of the Cross* were dismantled, and the building was restored to the form of a single, large room with apses, beamed ceiling, and Gothic windows along the walls. Here the paintings of the *Miracles of the Cross* cycle were redistributed, whereas the *Stories of St. Ursula* were moved to their present quarters (Room XXI) and hung in an essentially arbitrary way with stalls and benches from another church. A "period" setting was created also for the rooms still devoted today to small eighteenth-century works (Room XVII), with wall-hangings copied from contemporary fabrics and a small eighteenth-century doorway. More eighteenth-century doors,

probably brought from a palace in the Brescia area, and paintings by Pietro Scalvini and Saverio Gandini acquired in 1912, were placed in Palladio's loggia, where they may still be seen. As in Cantalamessa's arrangement, the nineteenth-century works and the works by foreign masters were eliminated; the former were relocated at Ca' Pesaro, the latter at the Galleria Franchetti.

An urgent need for the introduction of more modern museological criteria was felt in the 1940s, particularly in 1941 when Vittorio Moschini took over as curator. During the war Moschini and Carlo Scarpa hammered out a far-reaching master plan for the museum which called for the construction of a large building adjoining the nineteenth-century rooms. After the war, the urgent need to rebuild other Italian museums made such radical transformations unfeasible; nevertheless a start was made on the renewal that was to mark the end of the early twentieth-century museographical model. In the fifteen years between 1945 and 1960, the period rooms and wall-hangings, wooden baseboards and false cornices, were gradually replaced by neutral plaster walls, warm wood, jute, fustian, iron, and glass, all carefully selected and skillfully combined. An effort was

The Room of the Miracles of the Cross as arranged by Carlo Scarpa in 1959-60.

The room as arranged by Carlo Scarpa in 1950-52.

made to distribute the works in a more logical manner, within the limits set by the cramped quarters and obligatory position of certain large canvases; and in 1947 the *Miracles of the Cross* were moved to a room specially designed in 1940 (Room XX), next to the corridor leading to the Room of St. Ursula. The two rooms, with their closely allied decorative cycles, were subsequently joined by a small balcony. These early measures were improved upon in 1959-60, when the room with the *Miracles of the Cross* took on its present appearance. The exemplary renovation of the Room of St. Ursula (in which the pre-existent pseudo-historical reconstruction was done away with), and that of the eighteenth-century rooms (made over into a single, articulate space) were also completed in 1947. The year after, in the church, the pseudo-original decorative designs were removed from the walls, the roof was fitted with four new skylights, and fifteenth-century paintings were hung on panels as though in a temporary exhibition, with a view to respecting the extant architectural elements to the utmost. The years 1950-52 witnessed the renovation of Room I, where the windows that had been walled up during the nineteenth century were reopened, the late fourteenth-century fresco fragments on the walls were brought to light, and the view into the former Room of the *Assumption* was obstructed by a masonry panel on which Lorenzo Veneziano's Lion polyptych was hung. In 1950-53 a new entrance hall with the now-famous compass was created, and in 1955 work was finished on Rooms IV and V, where the small masterpieces hang alongside Giorgione's *Tempest*, now rescued from the theatrical isolation of the pre-war years. Francesco Valcanover, curator of the Galleries from 1961 to 1977, is responsible for the improvement of many basic services, including the fire and theft alarm systems. Valcanover also devoted much attention to the conservation of the drawings collection, which he regrouped on the top floor in a controlled climate and in special files. He provided the museum with rational and efficient warehouses, and he created a temporary exhibition space, dedicated to Gino Fogolari, in the area of the church opposite the apse.

In addition, Valcanover resumed the policy of acquiring new works, which had come to a temporary halt in the years just after the war. He brought in such works as Francesco Guardi's *Fire at San Marcuola*, Bartolomeo Montagna's *St. Peter and Donor*, Alessandro Longhi's *Pisani Family*, Strozzi's *Portrait of a Procurator*, and Jacopo Bassano's *Adoration of the Shepherds*, formerly in the Giusti del Giardino Collection, in addition to the *Madonna and Child* by Tiziano left to the museum by Senator Leonardo Albertini.

In the last few years attention has focused on the upkeep of the building, a review of all exhibits, and an intense effort to keep the paintings in good health. The panel paintings in particular were subjected to a systematic preservation program in 1978-79 which included disinfestation of the wood, consolidation of the pictorial surface, and, in many cases, restoration of the support. Nevertheless the Galleries continue to suffer from an endemic shortage of space, which in addition to blocking the development of the new functions attributed to the museum, precludes a truly chronological arrangement of the holdings. Suffice it to point out that 74% of the collections is not on exhibit at the Galleries: 47% is in storage, and the remainder is exhibited in other public facilities.

1. See S. Moschini Marconi, *Gallerie dell'Accademia di Venezia - Opere d'arte dei secc. XIV e IV*, Rome 1955, which the author of this introduction has drawn on extensively, and E. Bassi, *Il complesso palladiano della Carità*, Milan 1980.
For the history of the Collection of Drawings see also G. Nepi Sciré, *Storia della collezione dei disegni*, Milan 1982.

Giovanna Nepi Sciré
Curator of the Accademia Galleries

Plates

*Paolo Veneziano, Coronation of the Virgin,
detail of the polyptych.*

Lorenzo Veneziano, The Marriage of St. Catherine.

Nicolò di Pietro, Madonna and Child enthroned, with angels playing music and the donor Vulciano Belgarzone di Zara.

Jacobello del Fiore, Coronation of the Virgin in Paradise among the Evangelists, angelic hierarchies, patriarchs, prophets, martyrs, saints and virgins, detail.

*Michele Giambono, The Archangel Michael and
St. Louis of Toulouse, lateral panels of
polyptych.*

Jacopo Bellini, Madonna with Child giving blessing and Cherubim, detail.

Piero della Francesca, St. Jerome and a devotee.

Hans Memling, Portrait of a Young Man.

Carlo Crivelli, St. Jerome and St. Augustine,
detail.

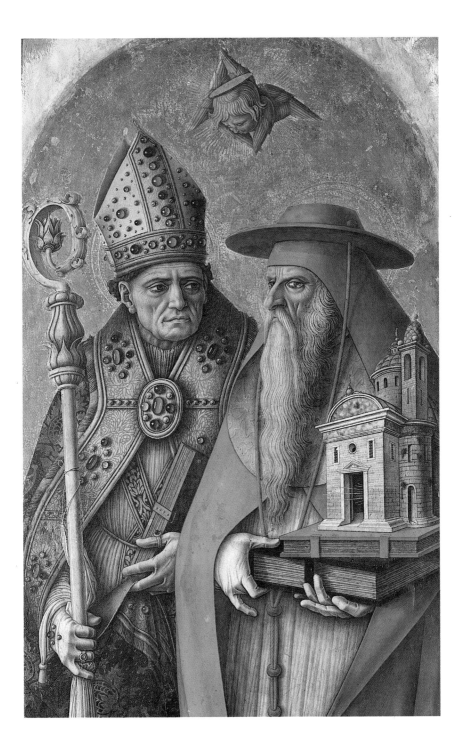

Gentile Bellini, Procession in St. Mark's Square, detail.

Gentile Bellini, Miracle of the Cross on San Lorenzo Bridge, detail.

Giovanni Bellini and the workshop, Triptych of St. Sebastian.

*Giovanni Bellini, Madonna and Child
enthroned between SS. Francis, John the
Baptist, Job, Dominic, Sebastian, Louis and
minstrel angels.*

Giovanni Bellini, Allegory of Changing Fortune.

Giovanni Bellini, Madonna and Child between
St. Catherine and Mary Magdalene, detail.

Giovanni Bellini, Pietà, detail.

Giovanni Bellini, Madonna and Child between
St. John the Baptist and a saint, detail.

Alvise Vivarini, Madonna and Child enthroned between SS. Louis of Toulouse (or Bonaventura), Anthony of Padua, Anne, Joachim, Francis, and Bernardin of Siena, detail.

*Bartolomeo Montagna, St. Peter giving blessing
and Donor.*

38

*Vittore Carpaccio, Arrival of the English
Ambassadors, detail.*

Vittore Carpaccio, Miracle of the Relic of the Holy Cross, detail.

Giambattista Cima da Conegliano, The Madonna of the Orange Tree, with St. Louis of France and St. Jerome.

Giorgione, The Old Woman.

Giorgione, The Storm, detail.

Tiziano, Presentation of the Virgin at the Temple, detail.

Tiziano, Pietà.

*Pordenone, The Blessed Lorenzo Giustiniani
and saints.*

Lorenzo Lotto, Portrait of a young gentleman in his study, detail.

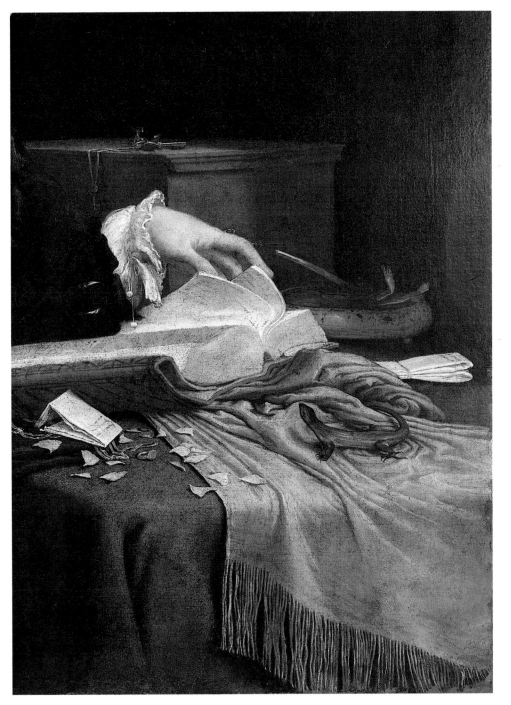

Romanino, Deposition and saints.

Gian Girolamo Savoldo, St. Anthony Abbot and St. Paul the Hermit.

Bonifacio de' Pitati, The rich epicure, detail.

*Jacopo Tintoretto, St. Mark frees a slave,
detail.*

Jacopo Tintoretto, Adam and Eve, detail.

Jacopo Tintoretto, *The Stealing of the Body of
St. Mark.*

Jacopo Tintoretto, Procurator Jacopo Soranzo.

Jacopo Bassano, Adoration of the Shepherds, detail.

*Paolo Veronese, The Supper in the House of
Levi, detail.*

Paolo Veronese, The Marriage of St. Catherine.

Domenico Fetti, David.

Johann Liss, Abel mourned by his parents, detail.

Bernardo Strozzi, Portrait of a Procurator.

Francesco Maffei, Mythological scene.

62

Sebastiano Mazzoni, Annunciation.

Giovanni Antonio Pellegrini, Sculpture.

Jacopo Amigoni, Venus and Adonis, detail.

Rosalba Carriera, Portrait of a Youth.

Giambattista Piazzetta, The Enigma.

Giambattista Tiepolo, The Translation of the Holy House of Loreto.

*Giambattista Tiepolo, The Exaltation of the
Holy Cross.*

Marco Ricci, Landscape with horses, detail.

Francesco Zuccarelli, The Abduction of Europa,
detail.

Canaletto, Perspective with Portico.

Francesco Guardi, Fire at the San Marcuola oil deposit, detail.

Pietro Longhi, The Dancing Lesson.

Alessandro Longhi, The Family of the
Procurator Luigi Pisani.

Catalogue of works

Note to readers

This Catalogue has been arranged in alphabetical order as a chronological sequence has not been found to be practicable for works in these Galleries.

Artists are indicated by name and surname, with pseudonyms in brackets.

In the case of 14th and 15th century works, supporting evidence is shown but comment on technique is omitted since identification of the pictorial medium used is often hypothetical.

The measurements quoted refer to height and width. Under "last restored" only the most recent restoration work is recorded. The heading "bibliography" quotes the catalogues of S. Moschini Marconi (S.M.M.) to which reference can be made for earlier bibliographical matter. Only subsequent items containing more up-to-date information or a new critical evaluation of a work have been added.

Division of the compilation of this Catalogue between two authors — the 14th and 15th centuries by Giovanna Nepi Sciré and the 16th, 17th and 18th by Francesco Valcanover — is the same system as is adopted in the catalogues of S. Moschini Marconi.

This Catalogue describes paintings exhibited in the Accademia Galleries at the time of publication, but some variation in their order and sequence may occur owing to work on the premises or on the pictures themselves.

Alberegno, Jacobello
d. before 14 July 1397

1. *Christ crucified between the Virgin and St. John, SS Gregory and Jerome on either side*
Panel, gold background, 45 × 55 cm (cat. n. 25)

Inscription: IACOB/US. ALBE/REGN-/O. PI/SIT at lower left

Acquisition: by bequest of Girolamo Molin, 1816; exhibited since 1852 only

Last restored: 1939

-Note the imagery of a Cross set in rock split to reveal a skull bathed in the blood of Christ; an ancient theme associated with the burial of Abraham according to the early Judaic-Christian cult, later found in 14th and 15th century painting and particularly in 16th century sculpture. The provenance of this work, which is the only one to be signed by this artist, is unknown. It reflects the influence of de' Menabuoi, Giotto and Altichiero (there is a similar triptych in a private American collection), especially in the fine painting and expressive vigour of the central panel. The Gothic elegance of the tall figures on either side recalls the work of Paolo Veneziano. Ascribed to the eighth decade of the 14th century.

Bibliography: S.M.M., 1955; pp. 6-7, n. 2; R. Pallucchini, 1964, p. 209; G. Bissali, 1980, p. 251.

2. *Polyptych of the Apocalypse*
Central panel: *St. John the Evangelist's vision of the Eternal Father seated in glory with the Lamb among symbols of the Evangelists "with six wings and all-seeing eyes", worshipped by 24 elders*; side panels: *The harvest of the world* (XIV); *The great whore* (XII); *The procession of the kings* (XIX); *The universal judgement* (XX).
Five panels, gold background: central 95 × 61 cm; side panels, each 45 × 33 cm (cat. n. 1000)

Inscription: CHI NO/N È SCRI/TI - SU / QUESTO / LIBRO / SERA / DA/NADI

Acquisition: 1951. The five panels became State property by Napoleonic

edict, then passed into the trust of "St. John the Evangelist". In 1838 the *Vision* and the *Judgement* panels were sent to Vienna whence they were returned under the post-war restorations of 1919. Displayed in the Museum of Torcello until 1948, they were reunited with the other panels, which had been stored in the Correr Museum since 1840, and finally were installed in their entirety in the Gallery

Last restored: 1952

Originally in the Church of St. John the Evangelist, Torcello, which was suppressed in 1810, rapidly fell into disrepair and was eventually demolished.

The imagery is taken from the Apocalypse, the relevant passages being shown on the small panels in Roman numerals, while the *Vision of St. John* refers to the fourth chapter. The didactic intention of the allegorical theme is clearly illustrated, while the figurative art of Giusto de' Menabuoi is reflected with chromatic sensitivity and with a vigour which is typically Venetian. The church of St. John the Evangelist was rebuilt after the fire of 1343, which year would set the date of this work in the second half of the 14th century.

Bibliography: S.M.M., 1955, pp. 5-6, n. 1; R. Pallucchini, 1964, pp. 209-210.

Amigoni, Jacopo
Naples 1682-Madrid 1752

3. *Venus and Adonis*
Oil on canvas, 54 × 74 cm
(cat. n. 743)

Acquisition: 1910, by purchase from
Antonio Grandi, antiquarian, Milan

Last restored: 1962

Like Sebastiano Ricci and Giovanni Antonio Pellegrini, Jacopo Amigoni has a prominent place in European rococo painting. It is not so much in large works, whether sacred or profane, as in small paintings with amorous and mythological themes, such as this one dating from the 1750's, in which the artist captures moments of fine poetic effect and of charm tinged with Arcadian levity.

Bibliography: S.M.M., 1970, p. 3, n. 1.

Andrea da Murano
fl. 1463-1504

4. *Triptych*
Central compartment: *SS Vincent Ferreri and Rocco*; side panels: *SS Sebastian and Peter the Martyr*; in the lunette: *The Madonna of Mercy with SS Sigismund, Nicholas da Tolentino, Dominic and Catherine of Siena*
Four compartments, of which the central one is canvas for easy removal: 152 × 88 cm; the others on wooden panels are each of 152 × 47 cm; the lunette's measurements are 80 × 199 cm (cat. n. 28)

Inscription: OPUS ANDREAE DE MURANO, lower left of central compartment

Acquisition: removed under the 1806 edicts, this work was stored by the State and in 1808 the central panel alone was sent to Milan, the others being reserved for this Gallery where they were separately displayed. With the restitution to Venice of the central compartment, which in the meantime had been transferred to canvas, the whole work was reassembled in 1883

Last restored: 1948

The triptych was originally in the Church of St. Peter Martyr, Murano, where each of the saints in the lower sections, St. Peter, the patron of the church excepted, was venerated as a healer of plague. St. Rocco is lifting his garment to show a swelling, it seems as a sign to the small figures of believers in the foreground that they should pray for protection against contagion.
The artist, who was an accurate interpreter of events that took place in his day on the lagoons, was one of the few to follow the disciplines of Andrea del Castagno. He would have been called to execute this work during a plague which broke out in 1485. Between 1485 and 1509 the church was completely rebuilt after being destroyed by fire in 1472 or in 1474.

Bibliography: S.M.M., 1955, pp. 41-42, n. 39; G. Nepi Sciré, 1979, pp. 227-228.

Angeli, Giuseppe
Venice 1712-1798

5. *St. Mark*
Oil on canvas, 146 × 78 cm
(cat. n. 1361)

Acquisition: 1807, from the Vecchia Accademia, Venice

Last restored: 1969

The artist was paid for this work on 14 June 1757, after which it was hung in the Assembly Hall of the Academy of Painting and Sculpture, Venice. Pittoni's *Annunciation* (see n. 216 below) and Marinetti's *St. Luke* (see n. 170 below) were displayed with it. Here we may note Angeli's resolve to up-date the forceful idiom of his master, G.B. Piazzetta, in a delicate and mannerised work which is notable for the wide use of differing colour tones of silver.

Bibliography: U. Ruggeri, 1983, p. 152, n. 61.

Antonello de Saliba
active between 1497 and 1535

6. *The Annunciata*
Panel, 47 × 34 cm (cat. n. 590)

Inscription: ANTONELLUS - MESAÑIUS - PINSIT, on border at base

Acquisition: 1812, following suppression edicts

Last restored: 1979

Having already hung in the Doge's Palace, this picture must have formed part of a group of works given to the Republic by Bertuccio Contarini and is probably the same as the "effigy of Our Lady" which Ridolfi saw in Casa Contarini in 1648. A copy of Antonello da Messina's *Annunciata* in Palermo Museum, and executed in 1476 or 1477, it was long thought to be the maestro's

own work, or indeed the prototype of the Palermo picture. Not until the end of the 19th century was it excluded from his catalogue to be considered as a near-contemporary derivation, if not a genuinely Venetian picture displaying motifs inspired by Bellini and Montagna. Their presence helps to render the assignation of this work to Antonello de Saliba who, it is generally recognised, stayed in Venice prior to 1497.

Bibliography: S.M.M., 1955, pp. 43-44, n. 41; C. Ciolino, 1980, pp. 217-218.

7. *Christ bound to the column*
Panel, 40 × 34 cm (cat. n. 587)

Inscription: ANTONELLUS MESSANEUS MEPINXIT, enscrolled at base

Acquisition: 1856, by purchase from the Manfrin collection

Last restored: 1979

The signature is apocryphal and by reflectometer examination shows, instead, ANTONINUS MESSANEUS PINSIT. The painting forms part of a group of works portraying the bust of the Redeemer with crown of thorns and rope at the neck supported by a column. The best is generally agreed to be a panel in the Cook collection at Richmond, but they all derive from a lost prototype which Antonello

probably executed in Venice. For a long while attributed to this maestro, this present *tavola* was assigned to the modest hand of Pietro da Messina in consideration of a signed painting of the same subject in Budapest. However, the high quality of the composition and its similarity to the *Annunciata* (see previous item) favour an attribution rather to Antonello de Saliba.

Bibliography: S.M.M., 1955, pp. 44-45; G. Mandel, 1967, p. 96.

Aviano, Girolamo
see Girolamo da Treviso
(il Vecchio)

Badile, Antonio
Verona 1518-1560

8. *Portrait of Friar Salvo Avanzi*
Oil on canvas, 65 × 57 cm (cat. n. 1318)

Inscription: M.D.XXXX XVI. KAL. MAIAS, at back of canvas at end of long written inscription and signature of artist

Acquisition: 1957, by right of pre-emption from the Counts Thiene

Last restored: 1958

In this early work, executed under Lotto's ascendant star, Badile portrays Avanzi, who was born in 1519, in the attitude and with the symbols of St. Thomas Aquinas to whose Dominican Order the young friar belonged.

Bibliography: S.M.M., 1962, p. 8 *et seq.*, n. 8; M. Azzi Visentini, 1974, p. 214.

Basaiti, Marco
works dated from 1496 - d. after 1530

9. *The dead Christ between two Cherubs*
Panel, 39 × 103 cm (cat. n. 108)
Acquisition: 1812, following suppression edicts, but not consigned until 1814
Last restored: 1979

According to the manuscript catalogue compiled in 1812 by Edwards, this and the two paintings below, with which it may have formed a single group, came from the convent of Santa Maria dei Miracoli, though its origins are not recorded there. Christ's body, represented in customary Venetian style and probably in accord with Burial Office conventions, stems from Byzantine iconographic traditions. As well as the influence of Alvise Vivarini, in whose studio the artists was apprenticed, certain similarities with Carpaccio's *Mourn-ing the dead Christ*, now in Berlin, are to be noted. A preparatory design for the work survives in the Uffizi Galleries.

Bibliography: S.M.M., 1955, pp. 45-46, n. 43.

10a,b. *St. James the Apostle, St. Anthony Abbot*
Panels, each 114 × 35 cm (cat. n. 68, 68/A)
Inscription: MARCUS (on *St. James*), BASAIT.P. (on *St. Anthony*), on respective pedestals
Acquisition: 1812, following suppression edicts, but not consigned until 1814
Last restored: 1954

Like the above, according to Edwards these two panels come from the convent of Santa Maria dei Miracoli. They must have formed part of a larger group in which, in the absence of any landscape features, a middle panel may have been inserted.

Bibliography: S.M.M., 1955, pp. 46-47, n. 44.

11. *The Calling of the Sons of Zebedee*
Panel, 386 × 268 cm (cat. n. 39)
Inscription: M.D.X.BAXITI, in lower left margin towards centre
Acquisition: 1812, following suppression edicts
Last restored: 1979

Executed for the high altar of the Church of Sant'Andrea della Certosa, this work is much praised in early comments. It is notable for the intensive dialogue between Christ and the Apostles, for its illusory space effects, and the unusual introduction of water in the middle ground, where the central feature of the landscape "focuses on a hill which looms up, isolating an acqueous mirror... then melts into the distance which is illuminated by the magical approach of the back lighting" (Parronchi, 1978). Despite these visionary features and other very fine details, this painting, which dates from 1510, adheres faithfully to 15th century figurative concepts. A smaller version showing some variations and dating from 1515 exists in the Vienna Museum.

Bibliography: S.M.M., 1955, p. 47-48, n. 45; A. Parronchi, 1978, p. 123 *et seq.*

12. *Agony in the Garden (Gethsemane) - SS. Dominic and Mark; SS. Ludovic and Francis*
Canvas on panel, 371 × 224 cm (cat. n. 69)

Inscription: MARCUS B... 1510, in left foreground

Acquisition: 1815, from the Church of San Giobbe

Last restored: now in course

The support of this picture has always been susceptible to movement resulting in the loss of some colour work and subsequent retouching, particularly in the figures of Christ and St. Mark, also the sky. Once on the right side of the high altar in the Church of San Giobbe, it belonged to Francesco Foscari (Doge) whose family names are repeated in those of the four saints. Referred to in early sources as a work of rare merit, it now eludes impartial critical evaluation owing to its poor state of preservation. While the figures of the Saints and Apostles in the foreground clearly reflect the influence of Giovanni Bellini, the background is of Giorgionesque inspiration, the harmony of the two main groups being fully achieved.

Bibliography: S.M.M., 1955, pp. 48-49, n. 46; V. Moschini, 1960, p. 362.

83

Basaiti, Marco (?)

13. *St. Jerome*
Panel, 54 × 42 cm (cat. n. 107)
Acquisition: 1816, the legacy of Girolamo Molin
Last restored: 1941

Attributed in the original collection to Basaiti who many times repeated this same subject. Although an attempt has been made to ascribe this work to Catena, it would seem more likely that it belongs to a late period in the life of Basaiti. Of small size, the picture was probably intended for a domestic interior.

Bibliography: S.M.M., 1955, p. 50, n. 48.

Bassano, Jacopo
see Ponte, da, Jacopo

Bassano, Leandro
see, Ponte, da, Leandro

14. *The Communion of St. Jerome*
Canvas, 193 × 241 cm (cat. n. 824)
Acquisition: 1919. Became State property by the suppression edicts and passed into the deposits of the Commenda. Sent to Vienna in 1838 and restored to Venice after the First World War
Last restored: 1948-1949

This work and the next one (15) were originally in the School of St. Jerome behind the Venetian church of that name. Recorded in 17th century sources as the works of Carpaccio, both are now ascribed to Bastiani and believed to date from the last decade of the 15th century. The repeated use of lengthy figures typical of this "painter of historical scenes" shows the strong influence of Gentile Bellini but without his sharp representative clarity.
Scenographic research reveals solutions adopted by Carpaccio in the latter's early canvases, as shown in *The Legends of St. Ursula* (see below).

Bibliography: S.M.M., 1955, pp. 52-53, n. 51; R. Pallucchini, 1958-1959, p. 106.

15. *The Funeral of St. Jerome*
Canvas, 211 × 264 cm (cat. n. 823)
Acquisition: 1919. Became State property by the suppression edicts and passed into the deposits of St. John the Evangelist. Sent to Vienna and restored to Venice after the First World War
Last restored: 1948-1949

See previous entry for the history of this work. The scene is repeated in more flowing style in one of the panels, now in the Brera, of an altar-painting of St. Jerome in Asolo.

Bibliography: S.M.M., 1955, p. 53, n. 52; R. Pallucchini, 1958-1959, p. 106.

16. *Donation of a Relic of the Holy Cross to the Confraternity of the School of St. John the Evangelist*
Canvas, 819 × 438 cm (cat. n. 561)
Acquisition: 1820, following the suppression edicts, but displayed only since 1852
Last restored: 1959

This painting is one of a cycle which adorned the Sala dell'Albergo or Sala della Croce in the School of St. John the Evangelist, where a relic of the Holy Cross is preserved to this day. The relic was given to the Brotherhood in 1369 by Philip de Mezières, Grand Chancellor of the Kingdom of Cyprus.
Originally there were ten canvases, of which eight came into the possession of these Galleries (see entries 21, 22, 23, 79, 161 and 256) one was executed by Perugino but suffered destruction and was replaced in 1588 by another by Andrea Vicentino which subsequently disappeared; the other by Mariscalco no longer existed in the time of Boschini (1664). The most detailed, though not always precise source, is a booklet printed in 1590 describing the miracles of the relic and giving the name of the artist and year of each painting discussed. After the Napoleonic edicts of 1806 the School and its assets became State property, but the pictures which the Galleries chose remained in place for some time. When handed over in 1820, they were shown periodically, being finally concentrated in a single hall as late as 1947. The picture, which shows the actual offering of the relic by Philip de Mezières, is imagined as an event taking place in the Church of St. John the Evangelist. As an outside view it provides factual evidence of buildings that were later to be modified or demolished.
We can see the old façade of the church in brickwork and, before it, the portico surmounted by a terrace with sculptures and burial site. One of the sculptures appears in a cartoon for a mosaic piece signed by San Sergio and now at St. Mark's. Through the main door a polygonal apse is seen with a polyptych over the altar which may be the same as in the painting by Giovanni Bellini (see entry n. 23). To the left, the round windows of the School are also noteworthy. The existence of the School with its Sala Grande raised two metres has been confirmed during recent restorations. It was heightened in 1495. This sets an early limit for the dating of the picture which the *Opuscolo dei Miracoli* (1590) puts, instead, at 1494.
Interest in this work is above all documentary and close analysis shows how remote it is from the phantasmagoric renderings of Bellini and Carpaccio.

Bibliography: S.M.M., 1955, p. 56-58, n. 56; A. Ballarin, 1978, p. 237; S. Mason Rinaldi, 1978, p. 299; J.G. Bernasconi, 1981, pp. 198-201.

Battaglioli, Francesco
Modena c. 1720 - Venice,
known record 1797

17. *An architectural perspective*
Oil on canvas, 131 × 56 cm
(cat. n. 461)
Acquisition: 1807, from the Old
Academy of Venice

Chosen in 1777 with other canvases from
the Old Academy of Venice for display
at the Sensa Fair, this is the painting that
Battaglioli executed on his nomination
to the Academy in 1772. In this imaginary group of buildings the artist shows
his skill at perspective and his ability to
enliven the scene with touches of colour
and an intensive use of light reminiscent
of Canaletto.

Bibliography: S.M.M., 1970, p. 5, n. 4.

85

Bazzani, Giuseppe
Mantua 1690-1769

18. *Adoration of the Magi*
Oil on canvas, 104 × 78 cm
(cat. n. 747)
Acquisition: 1909, the gift of A.
Salvadori
Last restored: 1938

This and the next canvas belong to a
series which is discussed under another
entry. With the *Deposition*, now in Leip-
zig Art Gallery, all are ascribed to the
1740s, by which time Bazzani had
brought his personal touch to the lively
rococo style he had learned from Cignani,
Crespi and Magnasco.

Bibliography: S.M.M., 1970, p. 136, n.
302.

19. *Rest in Egypt*
Oil on canvas, 104 × 78 cm
(cat. n. 748)
Acquisition: 1909, the gift of A.
Salvadori
Last restored: 1938

As with the above, this picture falls into
rhythmic elements of the greatest fluency. It is the work of a nimble brush that
delicately harmonises the colour tones
with a wavering background of silvery
and subdued lighting.

Bibliography: S.M.M., 1970, p. 136, n.
303.

Bellini, Gentile
Venice 1429-1507

86

20. *The Blessed Lorenzo Giustinian*
Canvas, 221 × 155 cm (cat. n. 570)

Inscription: MCCCCXLV / OPUS - GENTILIS - BELLINI / VENETI, at foot in centre

Acquisition: 1852, from the Church of the Madonna dell'Orto and permanently exhibited since 1887

Last restored: 1965

This painting was perhaps originally used as a processional standard by the church. Certainly it is one of the oldest Venetian canvases to have survived.

As Gentile's first work to be dated, it was executed nine years after the death of the first patriarch of Venice. It is highly probable that it depicts the same figure of Lorenzo Giustinian as was painted by Jacopo Bellini in 1456 and displayed at his burial, which "figure" was recently identified with a sculpture in the Lando Chapel of San Pietro di Castello, until 1807 the Cathedral of Venice. The searching analysis of the ascetic in so sharp a profile speaks of the artist's adherence to the School of Mantegna. It reveals his talent for the objective which was to make him the official artist to the Signoria.

Bibliography: S.M.M., 1955, p. 61, n. 61; F. Valcanover, 1966, pp. 9-11; S. Meyer zur Capellen, 1981, p. 5 *et seq.*; G. Gamulin, 1983, p. 34.

21. *Procession in St. Mark's Square*
Canvas, 367 × 745 cm, with two insertions of 72 × 145 and 70 × 167 cm in lower zone (cat. n. 567)

Inscription: MCCCCLXXXXVI / GENTILIS BELLINI VENETI EQUITIS - CRUCIS / AMORE INCENSUS OPUS, on sign at lower centre

Acquisition: 1820, following the suppression edicts

Last restored: 1960

This and the two pictures that follow formed part of the Miracles of the Cross series which adorned the Sala dell'Albergo or della Croce in the School of St. John the Evangelist (see entry n. 16). Two large insertions on either side of the lower front section probably correspond to two doors in a partition near the altar noted by Ridolfi (1648) and Boschini (1664), who speak of the picture having to be put together before being placed in front of the windows after restructuring work by Massari.

It shows a solemn procession in the square on St. Mark's Day and the various Schools that joined in with their relics. In particular it recalls an episode

of 25 April 1444 when Jacopo de' Salis, a merchant of Brescia, invoked and obtained divine aid for his son who had been gravely injured. The date and signature, somewhat touched up, match the indication in the *Opuscolo dei Miracoli* (1590) and other sources.

The first of the pictures painted for the School of St. John by Bellini, this is the best known one of the series, especially because it provides a precious record of the appearance of the Square before the 16th century alterations.

The Basilica sparkles with the original mosaics of which only one now survives. The big arches and the *Porta della Carta* still shine with gold and other colours whose existence has been proved during recent restoration work. On the left of the façade the houses of the attorneys, which were renovated in about 1514, conserve the appearance given them by the Doge Sebastiano Ziani (1172-1178). The Clock Tower can not, however, be seen as it was begun in the year of this canvas and completed in the early Cinquecento. In front of the Basilica are the pennants which were renewed by Leopardi in bronze in 1505.

To the right, beside the *campanile*, is the old Orseolo Hospice which was demolished about fifty years later to make way for Jacopo Sansovino's innovations and the construction of new quarters for the attorneys. The main procession moves from right to left over a rose-coloured brick paving replaced by the present grey and white of Tirali in 1723, while from the *Porta della Carta* emerges the Doge's retinue.

The fascination of this painting lies in its descriptive content broken into many sequences which, interesting as the episodic information and detail may be, is also of undoubted significance for the wealth of observation on costumes and the contemporary scene it illustrates.

Bibliography: S.M.M., 1955, pp. 61-63, n. 62; V. Moschini, 1960, pp. 355-356. See also entry n. 16.

22. *Miracle of the Cross on San Lorenzo Bridge*
Canvas, 323 × 430 cm (cat. n. 568)
Inscription: GENTILI BELLINI VENETI F /
MCCCCC, at foot in centre
Acquisition: 1820, following the
suppression edicts
Last restored: 1960

Originally in the Sala dell'Albergo or della
Croce in the School of St. John the
Evangelist (see preceding entry, also n.
16), where it hung at the centre of the
wall facing the windows. The legend is
that during a procession to the Church
of San Lorenzo between 1370 and 1382
the relic accidentally fell into the canal
and floated past other rescuers until it
came within the reach of its Grand Guardian, Andrea Vendramin. The enscrolled name of the artist has been repainted
but is quoted in the *Opuscolo dei Miracoli*
of 1590, by Ridolfi in 1648 and Zanetti
(1771).
This is another picture which is notable

as a documentary record of the Venetian scene with buildings topped by
chimney pots adorned with murals and
painted plasterwork. The calm green
water lends an atmosphere of hushed ex-
pectancy to a scene in which, together
with a colourful throng of onlookers,
Caterina Cornaro, her ladies to the left
and five kneeling figures in the
foreground, take part. Particular faces
have been identified with members of the
artist's family, but they could equally well
be governors of the School.

Bibliography: S.M.M., 1955, pp. 61-63,
n. 63; V. Moschini, 1960, pp. 354-355.
See also entry n. 16.

23. *Miraculous Healing of Pietro de' Ludovici*
Canvas, 369 × 259 cm; with insertion
7 × 151 cm in lower part of picture
(cat. n. 563)
Inscription: GENTILIS BELLINI / VENETI F,
enscrolled on altar steps
Acquisition: 1820, following the
suppression edicts
Last restored: 1960

From the School of St. John the
Evangelist (see entries 16, 21, 22). Shows
how Pietro de' Ludovici, a devotee of
the sacred Relic, was cured of quartan
fever simply by touching a candle which
stood near to it. The work has
deteriorated badly and, although the
signature is not an original one, it affirms
tradition. It is not clear whether the insertion in the lower section of the canvas corresponds with the opening of a
door (see entries 16 and 22).
According to the *Opuscolo dei Miracoli*
(1590) the painting dates from 1501.

It was probably the first to be executed
after the School petitioned the Senate in
that year to allow another 50 brothers
to be admitted in order to raise funds for
"continuing work on the large canvas
paintings that are being done for the
embellishment of the School". The
episode, for which the artist used his own
and his father Jacopo's preliminary
studies, took place in an interior which
may have been the Church of St. John
the Evangelist itself.
The triptych over the altar seems to be
the same one that Bastiani painted for
the Donation picture discussed in entry
n. 16.

Bibliography: S.M.M., 1955, p. 64, n.
64; V. Moschini, 1960, p. 354; S. Mason
Rinaldi, 1978, pp. 299-300; J.G. Bernasconi, 1981, p. 201.

Bellini, Giovanni
Venice 1430-1516

24. *Madonna and Child giving Blessing*
Panel, 79 × 63 cm (cat. n. 583)
Acquisition: 1812, following the
suppression edicts
Last restored: 1938

Long identified with a *Madonna* once in
the Monte Nuovissimo at the
Camerlenghi Palace on the Rialto. In this
connection Edwards in 1781 recorded
that a gold background had been added
during restoration, but no trace of this
was found when the picture was restored
in 1938 although a succession of coatings
was removed. Vertical background
blanks around the legs of the Child in
the centre, also a general rubbing away
of the paint layers, hampers critical

judgement. Together with the Brera
Madonna, this one has often been attributed to assistants working to designs
by the Maestro. However, a painting in
which Mantegna's influence is seen side
by side with the new Christian *pietas*,
characteristic of all of Bellini's Virgins,
may indeed be ascribed to this artist in
the years between 1460 and 1470.

Bibliography: S.M.M., 1955, pp. 66-67,
n. 67; G. Robertson, 1968, pp. 79-80;
T. Pignatti, 1969; A. Conti, s.d. (1971),
p. 241.

25. *Enthroned Madonna adoring the sleeping Child*
Panel, 120 × 63 cm (cat. n. 591)
Inscription: JOANNES BELLINUS. P.
Acquisition: 1812, following the suppression edicts
Last restored: 1938-1939

Damaged at the top, this painting which comes from the Sea Militia Magistracy in the Ducal Palace, is also badly worn over its entire surface. All the same it is a particularly important one and most imposing in spite of its small size. Here the artist re-states a pictorial theme of Bartolomeo Vivarini's (see entry 317) and develops an idea expressed also in the "Davis" *Madonna* in New York. The spatial insertion of the Lombardesque throne displays, however, quite another approach to perspective, and the Mother-Son relationship is itself a very new one showing the sleeping Child in an attitude similar to death in the *Pietà*. On comparison with *Santa Giustina* (Bagatti Valsecchi, Milan) it can be placed in the first half of the eighth decade of 1400.

Bibliography: S.M.M., 1955, pp. 65-66, n. 66; G. Robertson, 1968, pp. 60-62; T. Pignatti, 1969, p. 94.

26. *Madonna and standing Child giving Blessing*
Panel, 78 × 60 cm (cat. n. 594)
Inscription: IOANNES BELLINUS, on border
Acquisition: 1838, by gift of Girolamo Contarini
Last restored: 1938-1939

Among the Maestro's works for the period 1475-1480 this is one of the most significant for formal harmony. It is an early example of that interest in landscape which was soon to become a feature of Cinquecento painting. In spite of some modifications to the garments of the Virgin, the natural beauty of the whole composition and especially of the countryside in the distance remains unspoilt. It very probably provided the prototype drawing on which Bellini's workshop based the *Madonna and Child* in Santa Maria delle Grazie at Piove di Sacco and the one in the Contini-Bonacossi collection.

Bibliography: S.M.M., 1955, pp. 69-70, n. 69; L. Puppi, 1976, pp. 49-50.

27. *The Madonna of the Red Cherubs*
Panel, 77 × 60 cm (cat. n. 612)
Acquisition: 1812, following suppression edicts
Last restored: 1937-1938

Originally in the School of Santa Maria della Carità, this is a variation of those compositions that show the Child seated on his mother's left knee, an interpretation which may owe something to Carrara's *Madonna* in Bergamo. Of a later date than the *Madonna and standing Child* (see above), it comes a little before the *Madonna of the small Trees* (see entry n. 29). Mother and Child, whose looks are wrapped in tender union, are set against the background of a landscape opening to infinity and outlined by green, sloping hills that give the effect of that spaciousness which found fuller expression at the beginning of the following century. The lyrical motif provided by the red cherub seems to have been drawn from Bellini's *Coronation of the Virgin* in Pesaro Cathedral.

Bibliography: S.M.M., 1955, p. 70, n. 70; G. Robertson, 1968, pp. 93-94; T. Pignatti, 1969, p. 99.

28. *Madonna and Child enthroned between SS. Francis, John the Baptist, Job, Dominic, Sebastian, Louis and minstrel angels*
Panel, damaged at top, 471×258 cm (cat. n. 38)

Inscription: IOANNES BELLINUS, lower centre on step of throne

Acquisition: 1815, from the Church of San Giobbe

Last restored: 1971

Was originally over the second altar on the right in the Church of San Giobbe where similar pillars to those painted here are to be seen, but which display at their bases a coat of arms with an unidentified horse rampant. This was replaced by a St. Job by Lattanzio Querena. The great reputation which from the start this masterpiece has enjoyed is shown by its inclusion among notable Venetian works in Marin Sanudo's *Cronaca* dedicated in 1493 to the Doge, Agostino Barbarigo, and again in Sabellico's *De Urbis situ*, probably written between 1487 and 1491.
The above dates set a limit to the disputed dating of the painting at around 1496, in which year Antonello da Messina executed the altar painting for the Church of San Cassiano. Sabellico's citation has always raised problems as it seems to refer to a work of the artist's youth, which ill accords with the very marked coherence of the picture. It should perhaps be seen in conjunction with Sansovino's words according to which this was the first *tavola* in oils to

be commissioned from the artist.
The volumetric serenity, the neo-classical monumentality, the sense of profound space illusorily stressed in the original location by the recurrence of sculpted and painted pillars recalled by Robertson's photomontage (1968) and the felicitous chromatic effects are all unlike anything in the *Madonna degli Alberetti* of 1487 (see below), or the *Triptych* of the Frari, which although dated 1488, is thought to be slightly earlier, even if they share some figurative details in common with this work. The same is true of the altar frontal of Doge Barbarigo, also 1488, which has often been juxtaposed with this painting and also seen to display common details. A better comparison might have been made with the lost Ducal Palace canvases (1479), which Vasari saw in 1568. In any case, in the absence of any more precise data most experts accept that the work must have been painted shortly before 1480.

Bibliography: M. Sanudo, 1493-1530 (ed. 1980), p. 51; S.M.M., 1955, pp. 67-69, n. 68; G. Robertson, 1968, pp. 83-87; T. Pignatti, 1969, p. 97-98; G. Schweikhart, 1981, p. 471.

29. *The Madonna of the small Trees*
Panel, 74×58 cm (cat. n. 596)

Inscription: IOANNES - BELLINUS - P - 1487, lower central

Acquisition: 1838, by gift of Girolamo Contarini

Last restored: 1902

In spite of the much criticised restoration of 1902, which damaged the original coating, still partially seen in all its delicacy in the white neckcloth of the Virgin, this is one of Bellini's best known *Madonnas*, and the first of them to be dated. The two small trees to either side, which have given the picture its name, allude perhaps to the *Song of Songs*. Behind them one catches a distant glimpse

of two snow-capped hills which lend luminosity to Mother and Child whose attitude and expression speak for a new and very human majesty.
There exists a copy made in the 19th century before restoration. It is today in the American collection of Philip Burwell Roulette in Maryland.

Bibliography: S.M.M., 1955, p. 71, n. 71; G. Robertson, 1968, p. 92; T. Pignatti, 1969, p. 98.

30. *Madonna with Child between SS. Paul and George*
Panel, 66×88 cm (cat. n. 610)

Inscription: IOANNES BELLINUS, on border

Acquisition: 1850, by legacy of Felicita Renier

Last restored: 1939

The affinity between the Child and hands of the Virgin and the same details in the picture described above is most notable. However, the formal and compositional fullness demonstrate later execution in the last decade of the century.
Comparison of the head of St. Paul with that of the saint in Bellini's *Coronation of the Virgin* in Pesaro testifies to the Maestro's inclination towards softer features and warmer mellow colours in his later years. The strength of expression in the face of St. George, evidently a portrait of the original donor, does not exclude the possibility that this figure is, at least in part, the work of assistants.

Bibliography: S.M.M., 1955, p. 74, n. 74; G. Robertson, 1968, p. 95; T. Pignatti, 1969, p. 102.

31. *Madonna and Child between St. Catherine and Mary Magdalene*
Panel, 58 × 107 cm (cat. n. 613)
Acquisition: 1850, by legacy of Felicita Renier
Last restored: 1956

Among the most elegant and stylistic of Giovanni Bellini's works, and one in which the figures, presented in delicate, translucent blends, emerge from the dark background into a strong lateral beam of light. The same device, accompanied by a similar typology for the supporting figures, characterises Leonardo's work of about the year 1500. In fact, it was in March of that year that the Tuscan master came to Venice where Gusnasco was able to admire his portrait of Isabella d'Este. A version with variants, probably from Bellini's *atelier*, is to be seen in the Prado Museum. A studio drawing, possibly for the face of St. Catherine, which does not, however, seem to be Bellini's own, is in the possession of these Galleries.

Bibliography: S.M.M., 1955, pp. 73-74, n. 73; G. Robertson, 1968, p. 94; T. Pignatti, 1969, p. 101.

32a,b. *The Redeemer*
Two panels forming one piece: 33 × 22 cm (the *Redeemer*), 31 × 22 cm (inscribed section) (cat. n. 87)
Inscription: IOANNES BELLI / NUS MEPINXIT, on strip
Acquisition: 1838, by gift of Girolamo Molin
Last restored: 1938

Probably two halves of a *Transfiguration*, which subject was twice repeated by Bellini in versions preserved at the Correr Museum in Venice and at the Capodimonte in Naples. It may be that they formed part of that *Transfiguration* which Zanetti noted (1733) over the high altar of the Church of San Salvador, Venice, though the same claim is made for the Correr painting. The portrayal, so expressive of humanity, bears a certain resemblance to one in the *Baptism* of St. Corona in Vicenza and should therefore date from the first years of the 16th century.

Bibliography: S.M.M., 1955, pp. 74-75, n. 75; G. Robertson, 1968, p. 92; T. Pignatti, 1969, p. 168.

33. *Madonna and Child between St. John the Baptist and a saint*
Panel, 54 × 76 cm (cat. n. 881)
Inscription: IOANNES BELLINUS, on top border at centre
Acquisition: 1926, from the collection of Giovanelli di Venezia by special agreement with the State
Last restored: before 1926

This painting is of the highest quality in spite of excessive cleaning many years ago and marks a phase in the artist's development at the beginning of the 16th century. It is characterised by great creative freedom and by a new resolve to put the figures into a more spacious and luminous setting. From now on until he executed the altar-piece for the Church of San Zaccaria, Bellini's work was in keeping with, for example, the *Madonna del Prato* (National Gallery, London) and the *Pietà* in the Donà delle Rose collection (see next entry). This new development was for long an obstacle to ascribing such works to his hand. The picture, with its splendid background of a waterside city changing in colour to meet the line of the pre-Alps, does not, however, succeed in conveying the perfect fusion between landscape and foreground figures which the artist was to achieve under Giorgione's influence at the end of the first decade. Its most likely date is 1504 in which year Andrea Previtali painted his *Nozze di Santa Caterina*, now in the National Gallery, London, repeating in it the figure of St. John the Baptist.

Bibliography: S.M.M., 1955, pp. 76-77, n. 77; G. Robertson, 1968, p. 115; T. Pignatti, 1969, p. 105.

34. *La Pietà*
Panel, 65 × 87 cm (cat. n. 883)
Inscription: JOANNES / BELLINUS, on stones lower left
Acquisition: 1934, from the Donà delle Rose collection, by agreement
Last restored: 1935

Once in the Martinengo family, who had it restored in 1866 — not with the happiest of results — this painting is covered with a layer of pigment which gives it a golden tone alien to the bright luminosity of the original, as shown by tests on the paint layers made in 1978. Dating from halfway through the first decade of the 16th century, it reveals on close analysis of the meadows and the limpid colouring a certain western influence, in common with a trend of that time stemming from Dürer. The human drama is thus set against a more expansive background. No objective intention is to be attached to the landscape, the artist being content to introduce buildings of various styles and origins in wide-ranging synthesis. They include the pre-Palladian Basilica, the Cathedral and Tower at Vicenza, together with views of the Natisone at Cividale and the bell tower of Sant'Apollinare Nuovo in Ravenna.

Bibliography: S.M.M., 1955, pp. 75-76, n. 76; A. Ruggeri, *Giovanni Bellini, La Pietà*, 1978, pp. 93-97.

35a-e. *Allegories*
Five small panels: b, c, d, 34 × 22
cm each; a, 32 × 22 cm; e, 27 × 19
cm (cat. n. 595)

Inscription: IOANNES - BELLINUS - P, on
panel d

Acquisition: 1838, by gift of Girolamo
Contarini

Last restored: 1979

The first four of these small panels must
have formed part of an article of furniture
equipped with a mirror and bearing toilet
accessories: probably that "walnut table
with certain figures by Messer Zuan
Belino" mentioned in 1530 in the will
of Vincenzo Catena who left it to Antonio
Marsili. To these have been added a fifth
panel that undoubtedly came from the
Contarini collection, though doubt arises
that it may have been a similar work inasmuch as its original ownership is uncertain. Indeed these small items of "useless"
furniture became so popular that in 1489
they were made subject to a senatorial
decree against commissioning and con-
structing them. The figures that adorned them were therefore given a complex
moral tone, thereby confounding the accu-
sation of futility. Various interpretations have been made of the above, but
the generally accepted ones are as
follows.

a. Bacchus on a small two-wheeled
chariot offering a dish of fruit to a war-
rior, a pictorial device freely used by
Jacopo Bellini when illustrating *Sloth* and
Perseverance, better still, *Luxury* tempt-
ing the man of *Virtue*, in this case a war-
rior hero. Thus the allegorical allusion
here is to "heroic virtue".
b. The woman with the sphere in a small
boat surrounded by *putti* is believed to
allegorise *Changing Fortune*, or *Melancholy*.
c. The nude standing on the pedestal
with a mirror is recognisable as *Prudence*
or *Vanity* in traditional nordic symbolism.
The image is repeated in an engraving
of 1504 by Jacopo de' Barbari and in
a painting by Baldung Grien of the same
year which is in Vienna.
d. It is more difficult to understand the
allusion in the case of the man emerging in the coils of a serpent from a shell
supported by two others. In the past a
negative meaning has been given to it:
a symbol of *Infamy Unmasked*, of
Slander, *Falsehood*, but recently the more
positive interpretation of the *Virtue of
Wisdom*, as symbolised by the life and
generative power of the shell, has been
favoured.
Fine pictorial and lighting effects give
spaciousness to these small panels, whose
figures stand out with elegant sharpness,
making them unique examples of the art-

ist's iconographic skills. Estimates of their
date vary between the beginning of the
ninth decade of the Quattrocento and the
first years of the following century, the
latter more likely, 1504 being a date suggested by the figurative characteristics of
nordic derivation.
e. The fifth panel is an allegorical
representation of *Fortune*. Two amphorae
are balanced on two spheres and, in
keeping with a German tradition of the
late 15th and early 16th centuries, a
blindfold goddess indifferently offers
favours from one while pouring the con-
tents to waste from the other.
In a similar way Dürer, in an engraving
of 1501 to 1503, shows winged Nemesis
atop a sphere offering an amphora. The
coincidence with the allegorical content
of b), in which *Fortune* is seen to return,
would further suggest that the two panels
do not belong to one and the same group.
Their attribution to Andrea Previtali put
forward by Roberto Longhi is plausible.

Bibliography: S.M.M., 1955, pp. 71-73,
n. 72; A. Ruggeri, *Giovanni Bellini,
Vanitas*, 1978, pp. 34-37; C. Cierivia,
1981, pp. 126-145.

Bellini, Giovanni
(from his workshop)

36. *St. Ursula and four saints*
Panel, 64×45 cm (cat. n. 54)

Inscription: CATTERINA - VIGRI + BOLOGNA - 1456, at feet of the Saint on a strip with over-writing beneath which X-ray examination shows traces of another inscription: ORA DEO V. U.

Acquisition: 1816, by legacy of Girolamo Molin

Last restored: 1941

Traditionally attributed to the woman painter and Saint, Caterina Vigri of Bologna, the ascription to the younger Bellini, first advanced by Roberto Longhi in 1927, has found many supporters. However, the quality of the work and certain inconsistencies in its details call for a more cautious evaluation, pointing towards the Bellini workshop group, among whom the name of Lauro Padovano has been particularly mentioned.

Bibliography: S.M.M., 1955, p. 88-89, n. 84; G. Robertson, 1968, p. 51; T. Pignatti, 1969, p. 86.

Bellini, Giovanni
(and assistants)

37. *Mourning the dead Christ with Joseph of Arimathea and one of the Marys, the Magdalene and Filippo Benizi of the Order of the Servites (or St. Benedict)*
Canvas, 444×312 cm (cat. n. 166)

Acquisition: 1814, following the suppression edicts. The canvas was deposited, rolled up, in the Commenda until finally consigned in 1829

Last restored: 1964

Originally in the Venetian Church of the Servites (Santa Maria dei Servi), was described by Boschini (1664) as the masterpiece of Rocco Marconi, which view was accepted until the catalogue of 1903 associated it with Bellini.
The Maestro's authorship was later unanimously endorsed by the critics with the reservation that parts of the landscape and the figures of St. Monica and Filippo Benizi had received help from assistants. This is perhaps the artist's last attempt at another great altar painting. When examined closely, the extraordinary chromatic translucency, which recalls the paintings of St. Zachariah and St. John Chrysostom, seems to anticipate the *Inebriation of Noah*, now in Besançon and the *Feast of the Gods* in Washington.

Bibliography: S.M.M., 1955, p. 88, n. 83; F. Valcanover, 1966, pp 13-15; G. Robertson, 1968, p. 154; T. Pignatti, 1969, p. 110.

38a,b. *The Angel and the Annunciata*
Canvases, each 224×106 cm
(cat. n. 734)
Acquisition: 1907, the *Angel* by
purchase from the Langton Douglas
collection, London; the *Annunciata*
by annulment of its deposit at the
Church of San Francesco della Vigna
to which it had been ceded in 1817
Last restored: 1907 (the *Annunciata*)

These canvases adorned the external
panels of the organ in the Church of Santa Maria dei Miracoli which on their inner sides displayed a *St. Peter*, now in
the Academy deposits, and a *St. Paul*
which has been lost together with some
chiaroscuros from the upper part of the
organ. Boschini (1664) states that the
paintings belonged to Pier Maria Pennacchi, an artist of Treviso whose rôle as
agent in Venetian painting circles at the
turn of the Quattrocento is a controversial one.
Subsequently given various attributions
pointing to the Giovanni Bellini group,
and indeed to his hand alone, they were
recently subject to an attempt to assign
them to Carpaccio whose *Dream of Ursula* (see entry n. 77) displays a point of
reference, notably the angel. They were
probably executed to Maestro Bellini's

designs and then handed over to Pennacchi. In dating them the limit set by
the completion of the church in 1489,
with its floors of marble tiles visible in
the painting, would carry this work forward to the first years of the Cinquecento.

Bibliography: S.M.M., 1955, pp. 86-87,
n. 82; G. Robertson, 1968, pp. 96-97;
T. Pignatti, 1969, p. 103; D. Gioseffi,
1978, p. 97; V. Sgarbi, 1979, pp. 24-25;
G. Nepi Sciré, *Il pittore trevigiano...*,
1980, p. 41.

Bellini, Giovanni
(and the workshop)

39. *Triptych of the Nativity*
In central panel: *Nativity*; in the side
panels; *SS. Francis* and *Victor*. In the
lunette: *The Holy Trinity* with *SS.
Dominic* and *Ubaldo* (?)
Panels, gold background: *Nativity*
103×45 cm; *St. Francis* 127×48
cm; St. Victor 127×48 cm; *lunette*
60×166 cm (cat. n. 621)
Acquisition: having passed to the
State by the edicts of 1806, the
Nativity was sent to the Brera in
1808 and to these Galleries in 1891;
the two Saints were consigned
separately in 1834 from deposit in
the Church of St. John the
Evangelist, where the *lunette* was
stored until it passed to the Correr
Museum in 1840 and thence in 1923
to its present home
Last restored: 1948-1949

With the three other triptychs treated
below (see entries 40, 41, 42) it was
painted for the Church of Santa Maria
della Carità which was reconstructed in
the mid-Quattrocento. It was originally
located over one of the altars of the family
chapels in the *barco* (a structure
separating the raised choir from the body
of the church). Erected between 1460
and 1464, these altars, already adorned
with their relative paintings, were consecrated in 1471. Dismantled in 1807
after the suppression edicts, when all
buildings belonging to the *Carità* were
required to house the Academy, recomposition of the triptychs, prepared in the
1850s on a basis of the dismantlement
records, was not definitely started until

the end of the century. The number of
single pieces corresponds to the 1850
records and to Boschini's references to
the four triptychs made in 1664. But to
this day their recomposition remains
somewhat problematic as it seems that
the figures of the Saints do not strictly
relate to those to whom the respective
altars had been dedicated. Traditionally ascribed to Vivarini, they were later
attributed to the workshop of Jacopo
Bellini whose designs had been passed
down, and in particular to Giovanni.
It is therefore thought that they date from
the sixth decade of the Quattrocento. The
presence of certain archaic features such
as the use of background gold may be
due to help obtained from Murano craftsmen and to the wishes of the donors
themselves.
The present triptych was the altar painting of the *Nativity* chapel belonging to
Andrea Molin. Its lunette shows in plastic
relief effects the influence of Tuscan artists working in Venice, while the figure
of St. Victor is not without a sharpness
suggestive of the direct help of Giovanni
Bellini.
The *Crib* may be modelled on Vivarines-
que prototypes like the Prague polyptych
and the one at Conversano (see entry
321), but the Virgin is of thoroughly Belli-
nian style. On the verso of the St. Victor
panel are some drawings of profiles done
by Bellini himself.

Bibliography: S.M.M., 1955, pp. 77-82,
n. 78; G. Robertson, 1968, pp. 39-43;
T. Pignatti, 1969, pp. 35-36.

40. *Triptych of St. Sebastian*
In central panel, *St. Sebastian*; in side panels, *St. John the Baptist* and *St. Anthony the Abbot*. In the lunette: the *Eternal Father* and the *Annunciation*
Panels, gold background: *St. Sebastian*, 103 × 45 cm; *The Baptist*, 127 × 48 cm; *St. Anthony the Abbot*, 103 × 45 cm; *lunette* 59 × 170 cm; (cat. n. 621/a)
Acquisition: 1812, *St. Sebastian* and *St. Anthony the Abbot*; 1834, the *Baptist* from deposit at Church of St. John the Evangelist; after being sent to Vienna the *lunette* was returned by the post-war restitutions of 1919
Last restored: 1948-1949

See previous entry. Once in the chapel of St. Sebastian this altar painting belonged to Zaccaria Vitturi.
The recomposition of the three lower panels is certainly correct, as is seen in the continuous line of the landscape.

Considered the most important of these triptychs it is universally attributed to Giovanni Bellini, in particular the four principal figures. The penetrating features of St. Anthony the Abbot are somewhat marred by the restricted space available on the panel; they bear a startling resemblance to another by this artist now in the Royal Library at Windsor. But the general source of inspiration would seem to lie in Donatello's *San Prosdocimo* over the Saint's altar in Padua: a design which forges a visible link between sculpture and pictorial representation. Setting aside the gold background, the positioning of the figures, their neo-spirituality and the colouring of the landscape speak of an adaptation of the latest Tuscan and Paduan trends.

Bibliography: S.M.M., 1955, pp. 82-83, n. 79; G. Robertson, 1968, pp. 39-43; T. Pignatti, 1969, pp. 89-90; J. Stock, 1980, pp. 24-25.

41. *Triptych of St. Laurence*
In central panel: *St. Laurence*; in side panels: *St. John the Baptist* and *St. Anthony of Padua*. In the lunette: *Madonna and Child and angels*
Panels, gold background: *St. Laurence* and *the Baptist*, 103 × 45 cm; *St. Anthony*, 127 × 48 cm; lunette, divided at back into three parts, 57 × 188 cm (cat. n. 621/b)
Acquisition: 1812, the *Baptist* and *St. Laurence*; 1834, *St. Anthony* from deposits in the Church of St. John the Evangelist, whence the lunette was ceded to the Correr Museum in 1840; *The Madonna* was handed over to the Galleries in 1923 and the *Two angels* in 1954
Last restored: 1948-1949

Painted for the altar of the Lorenzo Dolfin chapel which was dedicated to St. Laurence and St Stephen. The inspiration, particularly as regards the three Saints, may come from Donatello, but the general arrangement is widely maintained to be that of the Maestro, while execution would have been left to his assistants. The actual hand of Bellini is more evident in the Madonna of the lunette and in St. Laurence than elsewhere in the picture.

Bibliography: S.M.M., 1955, pp. 83-84, n. 80; G. Robertson, 1968, pp. 39-43; T. Pignatti, 1969, p. 90.

42. *Triptych of the Madonna*
In central panel, *Madonna*; in side panels, *SS. Jerome* and *Ludovic*. In the lunette: *Christ in Piety between two angels*
Panels, gold background: each 127 × 48 cm; lunette 60 × 166 cm (cat. n. 621c)
Acquisition: 1834, the three panels from the deposits at Church of St. John the Evangelist; 1927, the lunette from the Brera Art Gallery to which it had been ceded in 1808
Last restored: 1948-1949

Originally in the Chapel of St. Ursula, which was granted first to Andrea Molin, then to Zuane Palestrina and after him to Giacomo Zorzi. It is perplexing that the group should lack an image of St. Ursula, but this may be due to the fact that in a first contract with Molin it was intended that the altar-piece should have five compartments with "Our Lady between St. Ursula...", and that this was later reduced to three. The paintings have suffered more than any others of the triptych series, but the lunette and the figure of St. Jerome are both seen as being nearest to the work of Giovanni Bellini.
The most authentic of the charcoal drawings on the back would seem to be those behind the two Saints.

Bibliography: S.M.M., 1955, pp. 84-86, n. 81; G. Robertson, 1968, pp. 39-43; T. Pignatti, 1969, p. 90.

Bellini, Jacopo
records from 1424 to 7 January 1470
d. prior to 25 November 1471

43. *Madonna and Child*
Panel, 71 × 52 cm (cat. n. 835)
Inscription: a versicle from an antiphon to the Madonna in the Virgin's halo
Acquisition: 1920, by purchase from the parish of Legnaro, Padua
Last restored: 1950

Rubbed and damaged in several of the painted areas and with the outline of an ancient frame still visible in the background, this is the work of an artist who was one of the key figures in the delicate process of renewing Venetian painting between the 1440s and the 1460s. The disappearance of the solemn full face effect of Byzantine origin from the presentation of Mother and Child, the three-quarter positions and the tender interchange of the expressions, by now far from the Gothic spirit, reveal this as a work of the artist's maturity.

Bibliography: S.M.M., 1955, p. 25, n. 22; M. Rothlisberger, 1959, p. 88.

44. *Madonna with Child giving blessing and Cherubs*
Panel, 94 × 66 cm (cat. n. 582)
Inscription: OPUS - IACOBI - BELLINI - VENETI, on original frame
Acquisition: 1829, when already in the possession of these Galleries, though title to ownership is unknown
Last restored: 1979

At the end of the 18th century this panel was in Padua in the possession of the Abbot Foscarini from whom it was purchased by the engraver Sasso.
Although once regarded as a precocious work of the artist, the highly finished technique with the cherubs in the background in graffiti work, the skill of the perspective shown in the parapet, in the projecting cushion and the book, rank this picture alongside a similar *Madonna* in the Burns collection (South Mimms, London) and suggest a date later than for the one at Lovere. The cherubs' heads are to be found in drawings by Jacopo of c. 1455 (Paris, Louvre, I 64), which provides a *post quem* date for a painting which was certainly executed during the full maturity of the artist.

Bibliography: S.M.M., 1955, pp. 25-26, n. 23; R. Pallucchini, 1958-1959, I, pp. 20-21; M. Rothlisberger, 1959, pp. 85, 86, 88.

Bellotto, Bernardo
Venice 1721 - Warsaw 1780

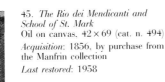

45. *The Rio dei Mendicanti and School of St. Mark*
Oil on canvas, 42 × 69 (cat. n. 494)
Acquisition: 1856, by purchase from the Manfrin collection
Last restored: 1958

This is one of only ten paintings attributed to Bellotto which are still conserved in Venice. It belongs to the youthful years of the artist, who was a disciple and faithful follower of his uncle, Antonio Canal. From the outset, however, Bellotto shied away from Canaletto's formal stiffness to fuse an appearance of reality with authentic observation. Here, against inky shade and intense sunlight caught in the hour before dusk, he defines one of the most fascinating, if little known, views of Venice: the Scuola Grande di San Marco and the Rio dei Mendicanti.

Bibliography: S.M.M., 1970, p. 5, n. 7; S. Kozakiewics, 1972, II, p. 20, n. 23; I. Camesasca, 1974, p. 87, n. 4.

Benaglio, Francesco (?)
c. 1432 - Verona 1482/1492

46. *Enthroned Madonna and Child surrounded by angels and cherubs between SS. Laurence and Jerome, Stephen and George*
Canvas for transferring to panel, 148 × 185 cm (cat. n. 617)
Acquisition: 1853, as deposit from the Padua Redemption Fund by permission of the Ministry of Finance
Last restored: 1889

The original location of the picture is unknown. Clearly derived from Mantegna's *San Zeno* polyptych, it has been attributed to both Jacopo da Montagnana and to Gentile Bellini. Owing to its bad state of preservation, which makes ascertainment difficult, a paraphrased text of St. Zeno written by Benaglio on the triptych of St. Bernardino should not be wholly accepted. However, an ascription to this popular promoter of Paduan and Venetian art at a time when Gentile's graphic imagery was a powerful influence deserves consideration, at least as an hypothesis.

Bibliography: S.M.M., 1955, pp. 64-65, n. 65; R. Pallucchini, 1958-1959, p. 70.

Boccaccino, Boccaccio
records from 1493 - Cremona c. 1524/1525

47. *Marriage of St. Catherine, with SS. Rosa, Peter and John the Baptist, the announcement to the Shepherds, the flight into Egypt, the visit of the Magi*
Panel, 87 × 143 cm (cat. n. 600)
Inscription: BOCHAZINUS, on strip at lower right
Acquisition: 1838, by gift of Girolamo Contarini
Last restored: 1979

Painted between 1516 and 1518, this is one of the most significant and complex works of the last period of the artist's active life. It was executed after his second stay on the lagoons (1511-1512) and after the frescoes for the *Vita di Maria* in Cremona Cathedral. Regard for Vene-

tian painting, especially that of Bellini, Alvise Vivarini and Carpaccio is very evident. Not a few ideas are taken from Carpaccio's *Sacra Conversazione*, 1505, Gulbenkian, Lisbon.
Adherence to the world of Giorgione is apparent and, after his Roman experience of 1512-1514, hints of Raphael and Leonardo. All these sources are drawn together in an archaic lyricism with an undercurrent of Ferrarese and Düreresque culture.

Bibliography: S.M.M., 1955, p. 169, n. 188; G. Panazza, 1965, pp. 6, 10.

Bonifacio
see Pitati, de'

Bonvicino, Alessandro
(Moretto, Alessandro)
Brescia 1498-1554

48. *Our Lady of Mount Carmel*
Oil on canvas, 271 × 298 cm (cat. n. 321)
Inscription: DIVAE MARIAE CARMELI / SOCIETAS, beneath the inscription on dedicatory label at foot
Acquisition: 1827, from the Church at Possagno
Last restored: 1956

Acquired by the Roman family of Ottoboni from Canova for the adornment of his Temple at Possagno, after the

sculptor's death this picture was obtained by the Academy in exchange for two paintings by Palma il Giovane. Dating from the early 20s of the 16th century, it is highly representative of the Lombard tradition of naturalism. Moretto applies his Venetian experience in gentle and subtle form to daily realities of Lombard origin to which the monks, women and children kneeling in prayer at the feet of the Virgin Mary all belong.

Bibliography: S.M.M., 1962, p. 145, n. 235.

49. *The Baptist*
Oil on canvas, 115 × 51 cm
(cat. n. 332)
Acquisition: 1856, by purchase from
the Manfrin collection
Last restored: 1959

As in its companion piece (see entry n. 50), the characteristic idiom of Moretto's younger years is seen in this panel. It is notable for its cool silver colouring and for the placid slow-moving rhythm of the figure.

Bibliography: S.M.M., 1962, p. 147, n. 236.

50. *St. Peter*
Oil on panel, 115 × 51 cm
(cat. n. 331)
Acquisition: 1856, by purchase from
the Manfrin collection
Last restored: 1959

In common with the previous panel the enrichment of the tonal values which Moretto derived from his Venice connection is softened by the calm pattern of brief, low key chromatic effects.

Bibliography: S.M.M., 1962, p. 147, n. 237.

Bordone, Paris
Treviso 1500-1571

51. *The Fisherman presenting St. Mark's ring to the Doge*
Oil on canvas, 370 × 300 cm
(cat. n. 320)
Acquisition: 1815, following the
suppression edicts
Last restored: 1958

Commissioned in 1533-1535 for the Sala dell'Albergo of the School (Guild Hall) of St. Mark, this huge canvas was probably painted shortly before 1545.
After a time in the Louvre, Paris, where it was taken in 1797, it was returned to Venice in 1815. The picture shows the fisherman who had helped St. Mark to defend Venice from the demons presenting the Doge with the ring which the Saint had given him in token of the truth of what he had related regarding that miraculous event. The scene is transposed by Bordone into a mixed architectural setting which conforms with Serlio's historical comments, while interpreting the courtyard of the Ducal Palace in fantastic terms. Perspectives, figures and buildings fill this resonant canvas with pleasing pictorial effects, rich in colour values and vibrant light, though modified in intensity by later varnishings that have yellowed with the years.

Bibliography: S.M.M., 1962, p. 70, n. 117; G. Mariani Canova, 1981, pp. 93-94; Id., 1984, p. 118 *et seq.*.

Bortoloni, Mattia
San Bellino 1685 - Bergamo 1750

52. *Glory of St. Gaetano da Thiene*
Oil on paper, 102 × 56 cm
(cat. n. 1337)
Inscription: at foot, indication of
proportional scale
Acquisition: 1966, by purchase from
Count Filippo Giordano dalle Lanze
of Turin
Last restored: 1967

Displaying the inspired fantasy of Bortoloni, particularly of his early work as a follower of Ricci and Pittoni, this scene typifies the artist's magnificent frescoes executed in about 1730 for the ceiling of the presbytery in the Venetian church of San Nicola da Tolentino.
Bibliography: S.M.M., 1970, p. 8, n. 12.

Buonconsiglio, Giovanni
(Marescalco)

probably born at Montecchio, Vicenza
in 1465 - d. between 1536 and 1537

53. *SS. Benedict, Tecla and Cosma*
Panel, 82 × 68 cm (cat. n. 602)
Inscription: 1497 ADIJ - 22DECĒBRIO /
JOANES - BONICHŌSILIJ MARESCHALCUS DA
VICENZA P., on label in lower left
corner
Acquisition: 1856, by purchase from
the Manfrin collection
Last restored: 1958

Part of an altar screen originally in the
Church of SS. Cosma and Damiano in
the Giudecca and partially destroyed
perhaps by fire between 1740 and 1741.
Ridolfi (1648) describes it as follows: "An
unusual piece with Our Lady seated on
high with the Child in her arms..."
Besides this panel, a second section was
also preserved which perhaps can be
identified with the *Madonna and Child*
at Warwick Castle. Both are described
in the catalogue of the Algarotti collection of c. 1776, according to which our
panel passed into the Manfrin collection
and was later acquired for the Galleries
by the Archduke Ferdinand Maximilian.
The inscription, evidently removed from
"the throne of the Virgin", where Ridolfi
saw it, was re-attached in the lower right
hand corner. Together with the Cornedo
pala, this is the first of the artist's works
to be dated. It reveals the influence of
Antonello and probably an acquaint-
anceship with the San Cassiano altarpiece, as well as benefiting from the example of the Bellinis and Montagna.

Bibliography: S.M.M., 1955, p. 140-
141, n. 149.

Busi, Giovanni
(Cariani)

Venice 1485/1490 - still living in 1547

54. *Portrait of a Man*
Oil on canvas, 70 × 55 cm
(cat. n. 299)
Acquisition: 1850, by the legacy of
Felicita Renier

While this portrait has been attributed
to Moroni, as being after Moretti, or,
again, to the Giorgione group, Cariani
is now commonly favoured as its author.
It is believed to date from c. 1517 at
which time the artist's inclinations were
for a Bergamesque style softened by the
colours of Giorgione's palette.
Bibliography: S.M.M., 1962, p. 104, n.
170; R. Pallucchini - P. Rossi, 1982, p.
143, n. 80.

Caliari, Paolo
(Veronese)

Verona 1528-1588

55. *Madonna and Child enthroned,
St. John the Baptist as a boy, SS.
Joseph, Jerome, Justina and Francis*
Oil on canvas, 333 × 191 cm
(cat. n. 37)
Acquisition: 1815, following the
suppression edicts
Last restored: 1969-1970

Painted in all probability in 1562 for the
altar in the sacristy of the Church of St.
Zachariah in Venice. Taken to Paris
following the Napoleonic requisitions and
returned to Venice in 1815. A work
which is among those that have been
highly praised by contemporary and
modern art historians alike, it is certainly
one of the greatest achievements of
Veronese's early years. Its incomparable
richness of sparkling, sunny colours
springs from an illustrious iconographic
tradition, namely that of Tiziano's Pesaro
altarpiece in the Frari.

Bibliography: S.M.M., 1962, p. 81, n.
135; T. Pignatti, 1976, p. 125, n. 127;
R. Pallucchini, 1984, p. 76.

56. *The Battle of Lepanto*
Oil on canvas, 169 × 137 cm
(cat. n. 212)
Acquisition: 1812, following the
suppression edicts
Last restored: 1983

Usually regarded as the canvas which in the Seicento hung to the left of the Rosary altar in St. Peter Martyr's Church at Murano, it may have been commissioned as a votive offering by Pietro Giustinian of Murano who in 1571 took part in this great sea battle. After recent restoration any doubt has been cleared up as to its authorship. The entire picture has regained its pristine freshness and the lower part is now extraordinarily evocative of a naval encounter which resulted in the victory of the Christian warships over the Turks.

Bibliography: S.M.M., 1962, p. 82, n. 153; T. Pignatti, 1976, p. 133, n. 166; R. Cocke, 1983, p. 239.

57. *The Supper in the House of Levi*
Oil on canvas, 555 × 1310 cm
(cat. n. 203)
Inscription: A.D.MDLXXIII DIE XX APR., on the left pillar by the steps, and on the right one: FECIT. D.COVI.MAGNU.LEVI. LUCAE CAP.V
Acquisition: 1815, following the suppression edicts
Last restored: 1979-1983

This picture was painted by Veronese for the end wall of the Refectory of the Dominican Monastery of SS. John and Paul to take the place of Tiziano's *Last Supper* which had been destroyed by fire in 1571. Of vast composition it had been meant to represent Christ's *Last Supper*, but a Court order of the Holy Office decreed that many of the figures were too irreverent for so sacred a subject and for this reason the purchasers and the artist were compelled to change the title to *The Supper in the House of Levi*. Requisitioned and taken to Paris in 1797 it was returned to Venice in 1815. Recent restoration work has brought out the groups of figures and the colour works, which had suffered in the Ot-tocento from extensive repainting and from serious changes caused by added layers of paint. It is now possible to appreciate the amazing symphony of colour notes and harmonies in the foreground and to see them against a setting of silk-like effects and architectural fantasies. One of the most fascinating pieces of decorative work to come out of Cinquecento Europe.

Bibliography: S.M.M., 1962, p. 83, n. 137; T. Pignatti, 1976, p. 136, n. 177; *Il restauro...*, 1984; R. Pallucchini, 1984, pp. 104-110.

58. *The Marriage of St. Catherine*
Oil on canvas, 337 × 241 cm
(cat. n. 1324)
Acquisition: 1925, after previous sequestration under suppression edicts

This canvas which adorned the high altar of the Venetian church of St. Catherine is perhaps the most highly praised work in Renaissance historiography. This comment of the Seicento critic Boschini remains famous: "One might say that to obtain these effects the Painter mixed pearls, rubies, emeralds and sapphires without end, and the purest of perfect diamonds." Marco Boschini's words are undeniable of a work in which Veronese achieves one of the highest and most pleasing moments of his rare decorative fantasy. Every occasion is made the motive for an enchanting song of colour.

Bibliography: S.M.M., 1962, p. 86, n. 139; T. Pignatti, 1976, p. 137, n. 183.

59. *Venice receives the homage of Hercules and Ceres*
Oil on canvas, 309 × 328 cm
(cat. n. 45)
Acquisition: c. 1895, from the Royal Palace, Venice
Last restored: 1939

This canvas, which was painted for the ceiling of the Biade Magistracy in the Ducal Palace, was moved in 1792 to the Sansovino Library and then, in 1810, to the Ottocento wing of the Royal Palace. Dating from about 1574, it shows an extremely clever use of perspective, as seen from below, and of translucent illumination through the colours, the figure of Venice rising against the back-lighting, the purity of her face veiled by a pearly grey penumbra.

Bibliography: S.M.M., 1966, p. 86, n. 140; T. Pignatti, 1976, p. 140, n. 205.

60. *The Annunciation*
Oil on canvas, 267 × 543 cm
(cat. n. 260)
Inscription: over the arch the coat of arms of the Scuola Mercanti (Merchants' Guild); at the foot of the columns the coats of arms of the Cadrabazzo and Cottoni families
Acquisition: 1812, following the suppression edicts
Last restored: 1969-1970

In October 1581 this picture hung above the door of the Albergo della Scuola dei Mercanti (Merchants' Guild), becoming State property under the Napoleonic regime. Thanks to its 1969-1970 restoration any doubt as to the true author of the painting was set at rest. The setting of the announcing angel and the *Annunciata* is indicative of Veronese's own admiration of the architectonic ideas of Andrea Palladio.

Bibliography: S.M.M., 1962, p. 91, n. 144; T. Pignatti, 1976, p. 161, n. 310.

61. *The Crucifixion*
Oil on canvas, 287 × 497 cm
(cat. n. 255)
Acquisition: 1834, following the suppression edicts
Last restored: 1969

Originally in the Church of San Nicolò della Lattuga alongside many other works by Paolo Veronese and his circle, this painting undoubtedly dates from the time of the church's consecration, which was in 1582. In a dark oppressive atmosphere the divine sacrifice unfolds in gripping recurrences of bold glimpses and luminous insights into a dramatic scene of suffering reminiscent of Tintoretto.

Bibliography: S.M.M., 1962, p. 89, n. 142; T. Pignatti, 1976, p. 158, n. 293.

62. *The Stigmata of St. Francis*
Oil on canvas, 256 × 432 cm
(cat. n. 833)
Acquisition: 1919, by restitution from Vienna
Last restored: 1929

Once part of the ceiling decoration in the Church of San Nicolò della Lattuga near the Frari, this work dates from shortly before the dedication of the church in 1582. Here Veronese achieves a well calculated play of overhead perspective and at the same time seems to tone down his palette to obtain a more *intimist* quality of expressiveness.

Bibliography: S.M.M., 1962, p. 88, n. 141; T. Pignatti, 1976, p. 156, n. 285; R. Pallucchini, 1984, p. 147.

63. *St. Nicholas acclaimed Bishop of Mira*
Oil on canvas, diameter 198 cm
(cat. n. 661)
Acquisition: 1817, following the suppression edicts
Last restored: 1939

Like the two preceding paintings, this one, which is damaged at the edges, was executed shortly before 1582 for the ceiling of San Nicolò della Lattuga. Here Paolo Veronese directs his attention to an elaborate arrangement of spatial and perspective effects and to quiet and carefully thought-out colour combinations of great purity.

Bibliography: S.M.M., 1962, p. 87, n. 141; T. Pignatti, 1976, p. 157, n. 286; R. Pallucchini, 1984, p. 148.

Caliari, Paolo
(from his workshop)

64. *The Assumption*
Oil on canvas, 464 × 310 cm
(cat. n. 541)
Acquisition: 1818-1821, following the suppression edicts

The central painting of the ceiling decorations in the Refectory of the Monastery of San Giacomo della Giudecca, this canvas passed with others of the same origin into State hands as a result of the Napoleonic sequestrations. An immense work, it clearly reveals the mark of Paolo Veronese's workshop, especially of two of its most active members, Benedetto and Carletto Caliari.

Bibliography: S.M.M., 1962, p. 96, n. 158a; T. Pignatti, 1976, p. 215.

Canal, Antonio
(Canaletto)
Venice 1697-1768

65. *Perspective with Portico*
Oil on canvas, 131 × 93 cm
(cat. n. 463)
Inscription: ANTON... 1765, at base towards the right
Acquisition: 1807, from the Old Academy of Venice
Last restored: 1985

As was the custom at the time, the artist gave a picture to the Academy after his contested election on 11 September 1763. He presented this one, and it is one of Canaletto's very rare paintings to have remained in his native city. The amazingly powerful style stamps on the mind every single detail of an imaginary view as a fragment of reality that wholly adheres to the truth in its figurative and chromatic values.

Bibliography: S.M.M., 1970, pp. 8-9, n. 13; G. Nepi Sciré, 1985.

Canova, Antonio

Possagno 1757 - Venice 1822

66. *The Wrestlers*
Terra cotta, 30 × 31 cm
(cat. Moschini n. 549)
Inscription: ANTONIO CANOVA, painted on base
Acquisition: 1807, from the Old Academy of Venice

In 1775 Canova won second prize with this group which he entered for the first sculpture competition to be arranged by the Venice Academy. Many students took part with the copy of an ancient plaster cast from the Farsetti collection. The original of the *Greek Wrestlers* is in the Uffizi Gallery at Florence. In this small terra cotta, modelled when he was barely eighteen years old, Antonio Canova established himself as the last great follower of 18th century Venetian figurative art with a work of lifelike vivacity which was both natural and spontaneous.

Bibliography: S.M.M., 1970, p. 226, n. 549; G. Pavanello, 1976, p. 89.

67. *Apollo*
Terra cotta, height 61 cm
(cat. Moschini n. 500)
Inscription: A...° CANOVA, painted on base
Acquisition: 1807, from the Old Academy of Venice

With this sculpture, today mutilated, Antonio Canova accompanied his request of 30 March 1779 to be accepted as a member of the Academy. It was unanimously granted at a meeting on 5 April 1779. In this splendid piece Canova shows his 18th century training in the soft, plastic quality of the body surface which seems to owe something to the style of Bernini.

Bibliography: S.M.M., 1970, p. 226, n. 550; G. Pavanello, 1976, p. 90.

68. *Pietà*
Clay, 21 × 34 cm
(cat. Moschini n. 552)
Inscription: A. CANOVA, carved on base at centre
Acquisition: 1911, by purchase from C. Quintiliani

On the death of Canova this clay model passed to his pupil Baruzzi who, on his transfer to Bologna to teach at the Academy there, gave it to Gardenghi, a canon. The latter's brother presented it to Cardinal Baruffi, Bishop of Imola, from whom it went to his heirs. In models like this one, executed in his later years, and showing him to be a sublime champion of neo-classical ideas, Canova nevertheless remained faithful to the freshness of his creative youth.

Bibliography: S.M.M., 1970, p. 227, n. 552; G. Pavanello, 1976, p. 133.

Cariani
see Busi, Giovanni

Carpaccio, Vittore

c. 1465-1526

69. *Arrival at Cologne*
Canvas, 280 × 255 cm (cat. n. 579)

Inscription: OP. VICTORIS / CARPATIO / VENETI - MCCCCLXXXX.M. / SEPTEMBRIS, enscrolled at lower left

Acquisition: 1812, following the suppression edicts

From the School of St. Ursula, today used as the clergy house of the Monastery of SS. John and Paul. In 1488 this fraternity of noble brothers decided to decorate its residence with "the story of Madona S. Orsola", relying on alms and, most probably, on the patronage of families like the Loredan. In all, Carpaccio, painted eight large canvases and an altarpiece (see entries 70, 71, 72, 73, 74, 75, 76 and 77) which bear different dates between 1490 and 1494.
Experts have generally held that the painting of these canvases went on over a longer period lasting until the end of the century, at least for the "Embassy" pictures (73, 74 and 75). On the other hand, recent restorations have revealed that they were probably at dates closely coinciding with the original ascriptions, while any stylistic discrepancies may be due to help obtained from assistants. Moreover, Mario Sanudo's statement in *De origine, situ., urbis Venetae* seems to have escaped attention so far. Writing in 1493 he recalls that "among the notable sights of the city is the chapel of St. Ursula at San Zuanne Pollo with its very beautiful historical scenes and figures". Indeed we think that by that date (1493) the greater part of the series representing the legend of St. Ursula, freely illustrating Jacopo da Varagine's book *Lives of the Saints* published in Venice in 1475, was already complete. In this version of the legend Ursula, a Christian princess of Brittany, accepts Ereo, an English prince, in marriage pro-

viding he will be baptised and, together with a vast following of damsels, will undertake a pilgrimage to Rome. In Rome the Pope joins them for the journey to Cologne where all are massacred by the Huns, which disastrous conclusion had been conveyed to Ursula in a dream. The canvases have been frequently restored and have at times suffered damage by being adapted to building alterations, as can be seen from the engravings of G. Del Pian. They were displayed over the altar, starting from the right *(Cornu Epistolae)* and so to the opposite end. This is confirmed by the discovery that a door once existed at the right of the chapel and that it corresponded with a gap in the *Arrival of the Ambassadors* (see 74). They were not painted in the sequence of the story and its episodes but started with the last stage of the journey and the massacre, perhaps because the Loredan altar and tombs had not then been removed from the other wall. In this picture the more spacious setting of some of the others in the series is lacking and the impression given in the limited space available is a cramped one since every effort is made to present the various events simultaneously. Recent restoration shows that the quality of the materials used is not easily recognisable, which fact heightens that atmosphere of unexpectedness which is part of the fascination of the story.

Bibliography: M. Sanudo, 1493-1530 (ed. 1980), pp. 50-51; S.M.M., 1955, pp. 97-105, n. 101; F. Pedrocco, 1981, pp. 74-88.

103

70. *Glorification of St. Ursula and her Companions*
Canvas, 481 × 336 cm (cat. n. 576)

Inscription: OP. VICTORIS / CARPATIO / MCCCCLXXXXI., at base of sheaf of palm leaves

Acquisition: as for entry n. 69

Last restored: 1982-1983

Much controversy has gone on in regard to the dating of this altarpiece which represents the glorification of St. Ursula who is taken into Heaven by the Eternal Father. In the presence of all who met her fate she receives the celestial crown. Although the year 1491 is inscribed the writing is not of the period. Instead, the strained imaginative effects suggest that a later date would be more correct and that the earlier one probably commemorates the year that work was commissioned.
It may therefore have been executed at the same time as the *Presentation*, originally in the Church of St. Job (see

entry 79), since two drawings, once in the Gathorne-Hardy collection at Donnington and today in the Ashmolean Museum in Oxford, were used for both pictures. Alternatively, work on the picture may have started in the earlier year and have been continued when the presbytery was re-structured in 1504, the three faces on the left — clearly authentic portraits of members of the School — being added at that time. However, recent restoration has certainly brought out the richness of the colours, and it would seem to confirm the inscribed date, suggesting that after the drawings had been pumiced the artist may have given his cartoons and designs to assistants for later execution.

Bibliography: see entry n. 69; S.M.M., 1955, pp. 104-105, n. 103.

71. *The Martyrdom of the Pilgrims and the Funeral of Ursula*
Canvas, 271×561 cm (cat. n. 580)

Inscription: VICTORIS CARPATIO/VENETI - OPUS / MCCCCLXXX / XIII, on base of column

Acquisition: see entry n. 69

Last restored: 1984

The column on which the family coats of arms of Loredan and Caotorta are crossed is the dividing line between the main episodes, to the left the massacre of the pilgrims culminating with the killing of Ursula, to the right the funeral ceremony of the princess. The focal point of the picture is the central figure — perhaps Julian, son of the Hun king — shown in the act of unsheathing his sword. The funeral cortège is accompanied by bishops, Dominican friars, nobles and members of the School among whom there are several drawn from life, though it would be rash to identify them. The most convincing one is the veiled lady kneeling beside the catafalque, almost certainly Eugenia Caotorta, wife of Nicolò Loredan, who was dead when the painting was made. Wearing the clothes of a zealot in which she was buried she appears to be something of an outsider in this setting. A most skilled composition of complex spatial surroundings in which descriptive details of Flemish style mix with idiomatic Umbrian and Ferrarese elements.

Bibliography: see entry n. 69; S.M.M., 1955, p. 104, n. 102.

72. *The Pilgrims meet Pope Cyriac before the walls of Rome*
Canvas, 281×307 cm (cat. n. 577)

Inscription: VICTORIS CAR / PATIO - VENETI/OPUS

Acquisition: see entry n. 69

Last restored: 1984

This painting represents the meeting of the pilgrims with the Pope before the Castel Sant'Angelo in Rome. The Pope decides to support them, baptises Ereo and crowns the royal couple. In dating this work expert opinion differs greatly. One guiding *post quem* factor is the figure of note in a red toga on the Pontiff's right. This is the Venetian humanist Ermolao Barbaro who died in the disfavour of the Republic in 1493 and could hardly be portrayed by the artist before that date. The procession is marked by brightly coloured standards and by the movement of white mitres and red caps, while the virgins wind their way in from the direction of the horizon and the blue line of the mountains.

The parallel progress of the processions calls to mind a similar solution adopted by Gentile Bellini in his *Procession in St. Mark's Square* (see entry 21) of 1496, which year provides an *ante quem* limit for dating the picture.

In it there are reminders of Van Eyck's polyptych of the *Adoration of the mystic Lamb* in Ghent, also some hints of Perugino who, in fact, was working in the Ducal Palace and School of St. John the Evangelist in 1494. A preparatory drawing of the Pope and two prelates is now in the British Museum in London.

Bibliography: see entry n. 69; S.M.M., 1955, op. 102-103, n. 99.

73. *Return of the Ambassadors*
Canvas, 297×527 cm (cat. n. 574)

Inscription: VICTORIS / CA...TIO / VENETI / OPUS, at lower left. On the base supporting the pennant on the left is an indication that the picture was restored in 1623

Acquisition: see entry n. 69

Last restored: 1983

This canvas is the best preserved of the series. It shows the return of the English ambassadors to their king with Ursula's reply. The person sitting on the river bank beside a small pageboy trumpeter is *Lo Scalco*, a steward whose duty it was to announce ambassadors with music to the Doge's banquets. Nearby, a young man advances with the insignia of the "Hosiers' Guild" *(Compagnia della Calza)* embroidered in pearls, while the other, shoulder on, is central to a composition in which Venetian buildings in all their details are borrowed to create a suitable setting. On the left one recognises the towers of the Arsenal, while one of the reliefs on the façade of the large central building is copied from a work attributed to Bertoldo. Note in particular the luminosity and vibrant quality of the colours.

Bibliography: see entry n. 69.

74. Arrival of the English Ambassadors
Canvas. 275 × 589 cm (cat. n. 572)
Inscription: OP VICTORIS / CARPATIO / VENETI, in lower margin towards centre

Acquisition: see entry n. 69
Last restored: 1983

This painting, which is the first in the development of the story, contains three scenes, each with different architectural features: the arrival of the English ambassadors at the Breton court and then the presentation of the marriage proposal of Prince Ereo; in the third, Ursula is in her room discussing the conditions with her father while her nurse sits waiting at the foot of the stairs.

The gap at the front of the canvas corresponds to a door opened up in the early 1500s which obscured the fine face of a pageboy on the right. Rough treatment damaged the figure which recent restoration has brought to light. A piece of the candelabra, which delimits the first episode and, in fact, appears in the engraving of Del Pian, has also been restored. Presented almost as a sequence of stage sets, this painting is perhaps the most complex one in the series: numerous portraits strongly reminiscent of Antonello's style have brought suggestions, just as numerous, as to whom they represent. All have been difficult to agree upon

but it is clear that they portray members and patrons of the School. One central figure displays the insignia of the *Compagnia della Calza* on his sleeve. The very large number of varied perspectives and the inventive freedom of the painter show that Carpaccio was well aware of the latest Renaissance devices in this field. Perugino's influence is seen in the building centrally placed in the background and in the series of arches on the left. Preliminary drawings are in the Library of Christ Church College, Oxford, the National Museum at Valletta, Malta, and in the British Museum.

Bibliography: see entry n. 69; S.M.M., 1955, p. 100, n. 95.

75. Departure of the English Ambassadors
Canvas. 280 × 253 cm (cat. n. 573)
Inscription: VICTORIS / CAR / VENETI / OPUS, in lower left margin

Acquisition: see entry n. 69
Last restored: 1984

Here we see the English ambassadors taking leave of King Mauro who hands them his reply to the King of England while the scribe, to whom he has dictated it, stands in the foreground to the right. The scene takes place in a Lombard-style hall resplendent in marble in many colours. Elegant artifices, the subtle play of light and shade, above all the decorative architectonic features add to the fascination of this episode. Although it is now worn, in some places the colour still blends with tonal effect, nor should it be thought that it has parted company with the underlying design which remains the structural foundation of this brilliant painting.

Bibliography: see entry n. 69; S.M.M., 1955, pp. 100-101, n. 96.

76. Meeting of Ursula and Ereo and the Departure of the Pilgrims
Canvas. 280 × 611 cm (cat. n. 575)
Inscription: VICTORIS / CARPATIO / VENETI - OPUS - MCCCCLXXXXV, on the base of the pennant

Acquisition: see entry n. 69
Last restored: 1983-1984

In effect, the central pennant divides this

canvas into distinct episodes: the prince bids farewell to his family before leaving; the betrothed couple greet the King and Queen of Brittany; finally, they board the ship which will take them to Rome. On the left, the capital of England is portrayed as a dark, tower-studded scene contrasting, right, with an idealised Breton city of walls inlaid with coloured marble reminiscent of Pietro Lombardo and his sons, and of Coducci. Two young

men at the centre represent the *Compagnia della Calza*, an association of young noblemen, the one who is sitting with a scroll perhaps being a portrayal of Antonio Loredan. The buildings have often been compared with the Reenwich woodcuts depicting the Knights' Tower in Rhodes and the Tower of St. Mark in Candia. But there is no doubt that Carpaccio designed them, partly from his inexhaustible fantasy, partly from other sources, perhaps supplied by Gentile Bellini after his journey to the Levant. This canvas is an immense choreographic vision overflowing with colour and invention, once again conceived in highly scenic terms with the onlookers crowding round figures some of whom represent members of the Confraternities. Preliminary drawings exist in the Duke of Devonshire's collection at Chatsworth, in the Hermitage at Leningrad and in the British Museum.

Bibliography: see entry n. 69; S.M.M., 1955, pp. 101-102, n. 98.

77. *The Dream of Ursula*
Canvas, 274 × 267 cm (cat. n. 578)

Inscription: VICTOR - CARP - F - MCCCCLXXXXV, in spurious writing on label at foot of bed

Acquisition: see entry n. 69

Last restored: 1984

This is the most damaged of these canvases, so much so that it was not until 1952 that it was displayed here to give unity to the series. While asleep in her room Ursula receives the visit of an angel who announces the martyrdom.
In spite of the serious colour deterioration and the loss of much original paint it is one of the most characteristic paintings of the Venetian Renaissance.

The light of dawn reveals all the objects in the room, one by one and each with its intimate significance: the bed and the bedroom slippers, the holy water stoup, the writing table and necessary materials, the myrtle and carnation plants, and then the puppy. In the Uffizi Galleries there is a beautiful preparatory drawing for the picture with the difference that it shows two sets of windows in the end wall.

Bibliography: see entry n. 69; S.M.M., 1955, p. 103, n. 100.

78. *Miracle of the Relic of the Holy Cross*
Canvas, 365 × 389 cm (cat. n. 566)

Acquisition: 1820, following the suppression edicts, displayed since 1830

Last restored: 1959

From the School of St. John the Evangelist, where it formed part of the *Miracles of the Cross* series (see entry 16), this picture shows the miraculous healing of a man possessed of demons, which cure Francesco Querini, patrirch of Grado, procured by means of the Holy Relic. In 1544, after hearing the opinion of "the wise messer Tizian pictor", it was decided to remove a strip from the lower left part of the canvas to accommodate a door to open into the new Albergo, then in construction. The gap was subsequently made good, as shown in a preliminary drawing by Albertina of Vienna for the figure seen shoulderwise with a small boy on the right. The miracle, which the patricians of Venice are watching together with members of the School and the *Calza*, passes almost unnoticed in a kaleidoscopic scene representing the city at one of its busiest points, as shown in a contemporary plan by Jacopo de' Bar-

bari. The bridge is still the wooden one of 1458 with a central section that opened for the passage of large ships. After its collapse in 1524 it was replaced by the present stone one.
On the left we see the sign of the Albergo Storione and a verandah that was much frequented by merchants. On the right is the German warehouse which was destroyed in the fire of 1505, the Ca' da Mosto with its porticoed ground floor, still existing, the bell tower of St. John Chrysostom's and that of the Holy Apostles before it was rebuilt in 1672. A comparison with the rigid, analytical realism of other canvases of the period lends further emphasis to the chromatic values and narrative power of this picture. Its most likely date is 1494, as indicated in the *Opuscolo dei Miracoli*.

Bibliography: S.M.M., 1955, pp. 96-97, n. 94; J.G. Bernasconi, 1981, pp. 198-203.

79. *The Presentation of Jesus in the Temple, saints and minstrel angels*
Panel, 421 × 236 cm (cat. n. 44)

Inscription: VICTOR CARPATHIUS / M.D.X.

Acquisition: 1815, consigned to the Galleries for conservation

Last restored: 1979

Originally in the Venetian Church of San Giobbe, where it hung over the third altar on the right which still retains the marble cornice with the coat of arms of the Sanudos who commissioned the work. Although much admired by contemporary sources, recent criticism has often seen in it an attempt to imitate the great altarpiece which Giovanni Bellini painted for the same church (see entry 28).

However, the enveloping light, the lyrical richness of the colours, the beauty of certain details like the stories from Genesis on St. Simon's cope, and the delightful inclusion of angels with horn, lute and lyre together refute any charge of imitation. Preparatory work for the two female heads to the left of the Virgin is to be found in a drawing at the Ashmolean Museum, Oxford, which was also used for the *Glorification of St. Ursula* (see entry 70). In this case inspiration almost certainly came from Perugino's fresco *The Finding of Moses* which was destroyed to give way to a *Last Judgement* of Michelangelo's style.

Bibliography: S.M.M., 1955, pp. 105-106.

80. *Crucifixion and Glorification of the ten thousand Martyrs of Mount Ararat*
Arched canvas, 307 × 205 cm (cat. n. 89)

Inscription: V. / CARPATHIUS / MDXV., in lower left corner

Acquisition: 1812, following the suppression edicts

From the Church of Sant'Antonio di Castello, destroyed in 1807 to provide a site for public gardens, it was displayed on an altar, consecrated in 1512, which the Ottoboni family had erected as a votive offering after an outbreak of plague. Here Carpaccio interprets the legend of the ten thousand Roman soldiers who defeated the Armenian rebels under Acazio in spite of the defection of their leaders. Betrayed by the latter, they were tortured and crucified on trees on Mount Ararat where they had taken refuge. In the foreground is the Persian king pronouncing the sentence of death. According to Vasari and judging

by the numerous copies that were made at the time, this work won wide acceptance. But the virtuosity required in striving to present so many episodes and details at one and the same time resulted in a confused and crowded composition for which the preliminary drawings do not exist.
However, it is possible to pick out features, particularly of landscape and sky, that are most pleasing.

Bibliography: S.M.M., 1955, pp. 107-108, n. 106.

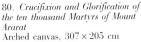

81. *Apparition of the Crucified of Mount Ararat in the Church of Sant'Antonio di Castello*
Canvas, 121 × 174 cm (cat. n. 91)

Acquisition: 1838, from deposit in the Commenda following the suppression edicts

From the Church of Sant'Antonio di Castello whence, after demolition in 1807, it was placed in the Commenda depositories.
The picture shows the vision of Francesco Ottoboni, Prior of the Monastery of Sant'Antonio, when during an outbreak of plague he invoked the intercession of the Martyrs of Mount Ararat who appeared to him in a dream entering the church in a procession led by St. Peter. As well as the organ loft, votive offerings and gilded polyptychs, we see the Ottoboni altar (see previous entry) which, instead of the *Martyrdom of the Ten Thousand*, is surmounted by an *Agony in the Garden*.
The work here treated could date from 1512, in which year the Ottoboni altar, still to be installed, was finished. Its attribution to Carpaccio, made in 1664 by Boschini, is accepted by art experts with some rare exceptions.

Bibliography: S.M.M., 1955, pp. 108-109, n. 107.

Carpioni, Giulio
Venice 1613 - Vicenza 1679

82. *Christ on the Cross*
Oil on canvas, 205 × 131 cm (cat. n. 1339)

Acquisition: 1967, after storage since the suppression edicts

Last restored: 1968

Originally in the Church of Santa Lucia at Udine, this altarpiece is an excellent example of Giulio Carpioni's formal precision in his younger years. It is marked by the well-defined execution of the figures, also by a cold, clear range of colours with which the artist reacted against the conformism of late-Mannerism. At the same time he displays in this picture a strong leaning towards naturalism, especially in the group surrounding the Cross.

Bibliography: S.M.M., 1970, p. 239, n. 585; ; R. Pallucchini, 1981, p. 208 *et seq.*

Carracci, Annibale
Bologna 1560-1609

83. *St. Francis*
Oil on canvas, 91 × 73 cm
(cat. n. 1189)
Acquisition: 1901, by purchase from
Alessandro Bedendo of Mestre
Inscription: illegible writing behind
skull
Last restored: 1955

Only recently recognised as having been
painted in the second half of the 1580s
by Annibale Carracci during his youth,
this work of the great Bolognese artist is
important as showing the influence he
had on Venetian painters of the Cinquecento in gaining acceptance for an
elegant refined style which is seen here
in the artist's superb treatment of the
landscape.

Bibliography: S.M.M., 1962, p. 273, n.
469; P.J. Cooney - G. Malfarina, 1976,
p. 94, n. 28.

Carriera, Rosalba
Venice 1675-1758

84. *Portrait of a young Nobleman*
Pastels on paper, 58 × 47 cm
(cat. n. 491)
Acquisition: 1816, by legacy of
Girolamo Molin

Of fascinating elegance, this portrait of
a young man painted in the 1720s calls
to mind the similar style of Fra Galgario.
It is worked throughout in a fine range
of greys and blacks against a fitting
background of open sky.

Bibliography: S.M.M., 1970, p. 13, n.
23.

85. *Portrait of a Lady*
Pastels on paper, 50 × 40 cm
(cat. n. 489)
Acquisition: 1816, by legacy of
Girolamo Molin

Dating from the second half of the 1730s
this was long thought to be a self-portrait
of the artist. Nor does its identification
as a portrait of Anna Carlotta Gauthier
de Loiserolle, wife of the painter Jacques
Aved (1702-1766), carry much convic-
tion when comparison is made with other
known portraits of that lady. The woman
here is serene and composed in the sure
knowledge of her position in life, and she
seems to be satisfied by the good looks
she has kept into her mature years.

Bibliography: S.M.M., 1970, p. 12, n.
22; G. Gatto, 1971, p. 186.

86. *Portrait of the French Consul Le Blond*
Pastels on paper, 57 × 45 cm
(cat. n. 490)
Acquisition: 1888, by legacy from Astori

This and the following pastels (see entries 87, 88, 89, 90, 91 and 92) form part of a series of portraits of members of the French family of Consul Le Blond who discharged diplomatic duties in Milan and Venice and was related on his mother's side to Vincenzo Omoboni Astori. Here Rosalba catches the good-natured disposition of the French consul.

Bibliography: S.M.M., 1970, pp. 13-14, n. 24.

87. *Portrait of Girl with ciambella* (a ring-shaped cake)
Pastels on paper, 34 × 27 cm
(cat. n. 444)
Acquisition: 1888, by legacy from Astori

With supreme mastery the artist captures the innocence and freshness of a girl dressed in her precious vest and holding a *bussolà*, which is a sweet Venetian pastry.

Bibliography: S.M.M., 1970, p. 14, n. 25.

88. *Portrait of a Youth*
Pastels on paper, 34 × 27 cm
(cat. n. 445)
Acquisition: 1888, by legacy from Astori

With a no less happy touch than in the above portrait Rosalba's lively brush reveals the gentle nature and sweet disposition of the boy decked out in the latest fashion.

Bibliography: S.M.M., 1970, p. 14, n. 26.

89. *Portrait of a Young Lady*
Pastels on paper, 55 × 41 cm
(cat. n. 496)
Acquisition: 1888, by legacy from Astori

This is another example of an exceptional ability to interpret the mood and attire of her subject in which the artist here discovers and presents the passing feelings, often inconsistent, of her contemporaries.

Bibliography: S.M.M., 1970, p. 14, n. 27.

90. *Portrait of a Prelate*
Pastels on paper, 56 × 44 cm
(cat. n. 486)
Acquisition: 1888, by legacy from
Astori

Rosalba Carriera shows this prelate in the proud spirit of his social position. He is perhaps to be identified as Abbot Le Blond. In her Diaries the artist records that she painted him while staying in Paris in 1720.

Bibliography: S.M.M., 1970, p. 15, n. 28.

91. *Portrait of Cardinal Melchiorre De Polignac*
Pastels on paper, 57 × 46 cm
(cat. n. 485)
Acquisition: 1888, by legacy from
Astori

The Cardinal, who was one of the artist's clients and a friend of the Le Blonds, was probably painted during his brief stay in Venice in 1732 when he had completed a mission to Rome and was on his way back to Paris. The strong will of this high prelate is recorded with the most admirable veracity in pastels.

Bibliography: S.M.M., 1970, p. 15, n. 29; G. Gatto, 1971, p. 186.

92. *A Self-portrait*
Pastels on paper, 31 × 25 cm
(cat. n. 907)
Acquisition: 1927, by pre-emptive
right from the Venetian firm of Naya

Recorded in the Dal Zotto collection as a self-portrait of the artist in advanced years. Here Rosalba realistically presents herself in physical decline with grey hair, tired lines in the face and eyes bereft of interest, a sign that her sight would soon fail her.

Bibliography: S.M.M., 1970, pp. 15-16, n. 30; B. Sani, 1977, p. 124; E. Martini, 1983, p. 500, n. 160.

Catarino
recorded in Venice from 1362 to
1382

93. *The Coronation of the Virgin,
with angels*
Panel, gold background, 89 × 58 cm
(cat. n. 16)
Inscription: MCCCLXXV · ⅮMEXE · Ɒ /
MARCO · CHATARINUS · PINXIT, at centre
of step to throne
Acquisition: 1877, by purchase from
Count Vincenzo Galli
Last restored: 1948

The original whereabouts of this work,
which is supposed to have been the central feature of a large group, is unknown.
The iconographical source may owe
something to Paolo Veneziano whose rich
chromatic effects are to be seen here, but
the work demonstrates a less stylish hand
than his, although one which is both
natural and effective. The painting of the
angels recalls work by Lorenzo Veneziano and other Veronese contemporaries.

Bibliography: S.M.M., 1955, p. 8, n. 4;
R. Pallucchini, 1964, p. 197.

111

94. *Triptych*
In the central panel: *The Coronation
of the Virgin, with angels;* in side
panels: *SS. Lucia and Nicola da
Tolentino*
Panels, gold background: central,
105 × 58 cm; side, each 96 × 28
(cat. n. 702)
Inscription: CHATA PINXIT, signed on
step of throne
Acquisition: 1902, by purchase from
Tommaso Mazzoli of Venice
Last restored: 1951

The original whereabouts of this triptych
is also unknown, but it was probably
painted after *The Coronation* of 1375
(see previous entry), as is suggested by
the very natural appearance of the
figures, the elegance of St. Lucia which
Lorenzo Veneziano may have inspired,
and the severe expression of St. Nicholas.

Bibliography: S.M.M., 1955, pp. 7-8, n.
3; R. Pallucchini, 1964, p. 198.

Chiozzotto
see Marinetti, Antonio

Cima, Giambattista
da Conegliano
Conegliano 1459/1460 - 1517/1518

95. *Christ in agony supported by the
Madonna, Nicodemus and St. John,
with the Marys*
Panel, 73 × 115 cm (cat. n. 604)
Inscription: IOANNIS BAPTISTE
CONEGANENSIS OPUS, lower edge
towards right
Acquisition: 1850, by legacy of
Felicita Renier
Last restored: 1950

A work of the artist's youth dating from
about 1490, as the lack of any surrounding detail seems to indicate. It is unknown
where the picture came from. While supporting evidence is weak, it is supposed,
however, to have been in the chapter
house of the Monastery of Mount Carmel
at Murano. Borrowings from Alvise
Vivarini, Antonello and Giovanni Bellini,
in particular from the latter's *Dead Christ
with angels*, now in the Museo Civico at
Rimini, are to be noted.

Bibliography: S.M.M., 1955, pp.
111-112, n. 112; L. Menegazzi, 1981,
pp. 95-96; P. Humfrey, 1983, p. 151.

96. *The Madonna of the Orange Tree, with St. Louis of France and St. Jerome*
Scalloped panel, 212 × 139 cm (cat. n. 815)

Inscription: IOA - BAPT - CONEGL -. signature on scroll at foot of Virgin

Acquisition: 1919. After becoming State property following the suppression edicts was sent to Vienna in 1816, returned to Venice after the First World War and assigned to these Galleries

Last restored: 1979

Coming originally from the Church of Santa Chiara in Murano this panel is a variation of *Rest on the Flight into Egypt*, as is shown by the presence of St. Joseph, small in the background with ass to the left of the orange tree which gives its name to the picture in allusion to the Virgin. The similarity of the central group to that of the *Sacred Conversation* in Lisbon suggests that the date of the work falls between 1495 and 1497. Clarity of design, the crystal purity of the colour, the attractive countryside dominated by a castle reminiscent of that of San Salvatore di Collalto combine to make this one of the most felicitous scenes painted by Cima.

Bibliography: S.M.M., 1955, pp. 113-114, n. 113; L. Menegazzi, 1981, pp. 100-101; P. Humfrey, 1983, pp. 153-154.

97. *Madonna and Child Enthroned, with minstrel angels, SS. Anthony Abbot, Sebastian, Lucia, Nicholas, George and Catherine*
Panel, 412 × 210 cm (cat. n. 36)

Acquisition: 1812, following the suppression edicts

Last restored: 1982

Painted for the Church of Santa Maria della Carità where its place was over a marble altar commissioned by Giorgio Dragan from the Milanese Cristoforo Solari. With its close affinity to the Miglionic polyptych, which displays greater maturity of style and is dated 1499, the date here should fall between 1496 and 1499 when the client Dragan died. It is probable that illusory space effects linked the marble cornice with the false architecture of the altarpiece, an unusual feature of this artist's work. Yellowed painting and retouching obstruct close inspection and make it difficult to guess at the original colour values. But the design, as revealed by radiographic examination, is a particularly clear one and shows that the face of St. Catherine was in the first place to have been in profile but was subsequently altered.

Bibliography: S.M.M., 1955, pp. 113-114, n. 114; L. Menegazzi, 1981, pp. 102-103; P. Humfrey, 1983, pp. 147-150; *Riflettoscopia...*, 1984, pp. 42-47.

98. *The Doubts of St. Thomas and St. Magnus Bishop*
Scalloped panel, 215 × 151 cm (cat. n. 611)

Acquisition: 1829. After becoming State property by the suppression edicts the picture was consigned to the Commenda deposits and remained there until it was given to these Galleries

Last restored: 1979

This picture, once over the altar of the Scuola dei Mureri at San Samuele whose patrons were St. Thomas and St. Magnus, has long been considered one of the most important works that Cima undertook in Venice during the early years of the Cinquecento. It was painted immediately after another of the same subject done for the Scuola di San Tommaso in Portogruaro and dated 1504. In a splendid study of light and shade the figures are sharply defined against the motionless surroundings of a clear sky and the distant village behind them. A beautifully balanced composition and the truly classical dignity of the picture are wholly unaffected by the changes in colour tone that Giorgione was at that time introducing.

Bibliography: S.M.M., 1955, pp. 114-115, n. 115; L. Menegazzi, 1981, pp. 118-119; P. Humfrey, 1983, pp. 151-152.

99. *Madonna with Child between John the Baptist and St. Paul*
Panel, 82 × 122 cm (cat. n. 603)
Acquisition: 1838, by gift of Girolamo Contarini
Last restored: 1979

Perhaps the same picture that Riudolfi saw and described in the house of Bartolo Dolfin, since other pictures that were left by him to the Contarinis were given to these Galleries. Ascribed to a date halfway through the first decade of the Cinquecento and to the influence of Giovanni Bellini, it has been said to reflect a certain weariness on the part of the artist. But the firmness of the touch and the quiet composure of the figures are unquestionable. The ornament on the hilt of the sword is probably derived from a plaquette by Maderno.

Bibliography: S.M.M., 1955, p. 115, n. 116; L. Menegazzi, 1981, pp.133-134; P. Humfrey, 1983, p. 151.

Cima, Giambattista da Conegliano
(from his workshop)

100 a, b. *St. Augustine and St. Jerome*
Panels, 74 × 26 cm and 74 × 25 cm (cat. ns 72,73)
Acquisition: 1812, following the suppression edicts, but in fact received by these Galleries only in 1814
Last restored: 1979

Originally in the Venetian convent of Santa Giustina, these two panels formed part of a polyptych which was split up after the suppression edicts. Three panels displaying St. Giustina, St. Gregory and St. Ambrose were sent in 1811 to the Brera Gallery in Milan, where they still are. All are products of Cima's workshop, this one of St. Jerome being a rather tired version of the same figure painted by Cima in 1499 for his polyptych at Miglionico.

Bibliography: S.M.M., 1955, pp. 120-121, n. 121; L. Menegazzi, 1981, p. 143; P. Humfrey, 1983, p. 150.

Cincani, Bartolomeo
(Montagna, Bartolomeo)
probably born in Vicenza
records from 1459 - Vicenza 1523

101. *St. Peter, giving blessing and Donor*
Panel, 60 × 39 cm (cat. n. 1343)
Inscription: ESTO FIDELIS, on scroll held in dog's mouth
Acquisition: 1971, by purchase from the Novello Papafava collection of the Carraresi family of Padua
Last restored: 1978

Described by Crowe and Cavalcaselle as being in the Papafava collection in Padua since 1871, then acquired by the State through a pre-emption claim against Robert Powler of Florence. It was Berenson who in 1957 was first to attribute the picture to Montagna, an opinion widely endorsed by contemporary experts who agree that there is a close stylistic and iconographic relationship with other works of this artist, especially with the frescoes in the Veronese church of SS. Nazaro and Celso which he painted between 1504 and 1506. As a work of about the same period, we note a remarkable harmony between the figure, the architecture and the landscape. Here an underlying "antonellism" enriched by hints of the Bellinis is apparent, particularly in the charming glimpses of the Venetian mainland with the façade of Vicenza Cathedral and the Arena at Pola recognisable among buildings taken from various sources.

Bibliography: A. Rizzi, 1978, pp. 41-49.

102. *The Madonna Enthroned, SS. Sebastian and Jerome*, in the medallions, top left and right, *Adam and Eve*
Panel, 216 × 162 cm (cat. n. 80)
Inscription: OPUS BARTHOLOMEI MONTAGNA, on step of throne, with signature rewritten
Acquisition: 1816, by legacy of Girolamo Molin
Last restored: 1979

Painted for the Church of San Sebastian in Verona where it remained until 1716, this is the last work of the artist during his stay in Verona. Although the composition of the whole may be lacking in harmony of detail, the picture is an admirable one. The generally accepted date is 1507, the year given by 18th century sources but today no longer visible. A very fine preliminary design for the Madonna is in Lille Museum, while various studies for St. Sebastian exist in the Estense Art Gallery in Modena.

Bibliography: S.M.M., 1955, p. 144, n. 154; L. Puppi, 1962, pp. 128-129.

Crespi, Luigi
Bologna c. 1709 - c. 1779

103. *A Self-portrait*
Oil on canvas, 103 × 95 cm (cat. n. 482)
Inscription: ALOYSIUS CANON. CRISPI BON. PROFESS.; ACCAD. FLORENTIA PARMEN ATQ.VENET. PINXIT ANNO 1778
Acquisition: 1807, from the Old Academy of Venice
Last restored: 1859

This self-portrait was given to the Venice Academy shortly after annexation to the Institute, on December 8, 1776, by the Canonico, Luigi Crespi, son of Giuseppe Maria. A clear connection is to be seen with the latter "still life" of the Bologna Music Conservatory in the book shelves with some volumes by the same Crespi. They include the third volume of *Felsina pittrice*, *Pitture di Brescia*, *La Certosa di Bologna*, and others.

Bibliography: S.M.M., 1970, p. 139, n. 310.

Crivelli, Carlo
Venice 1430/1435
d. between 1494 and 1500

104. *St. Jerome and St. Augustine*
Panel, 187 × 72 cm (cat. n. 103)
SS. Peter and Paul
Fragmentary panel, 217 × 47 cm (cat. n. 103/A)
Acquisition: the first in 1883 by exchange with the Brera Gallery; the second in 1895 by purchase from Count Gian Astolfo Servanzi Gollio di Sansevero
Last restored: 1979

Originally in the Cathedral of Camerino to either side of the *Madonna della Candeletta*, today in the Brera, with which it made up a triptych, it is supposed to have been surmounted by a *Crucified Christ between St. John the Evangelist and Mary Magdalene*, this too being now in the Brera. When Camerino Cathedral was destroyed by earthquake in 1799 part of the group was given to the Dominicans for one of their churches, whence *the Madonna, Crucifixion* and *SS. Jerome and Augustine* were taken to Milan in 1811. The two Saints

were then passed on to these Galleries. The panel of *SS. Peter and Paul* was probably retrieved from beneath the rubble in 1830 and later to the State. However graphic the expression of the saints may be, especially Jerome and Augustine, who are shown with "an anxious, ductile, even harrowing look" (Longhi, 1946), that expression is in strong contrast with the tired, formal preciosity of the Virgin. Yet the three works undoubtedly belong to a single group, as confirmed not only by their recorded history but also by the measurements and by the repetition of the same parapet. The term "eques", which the solitary, "surreal" artist called himself when signing the central panel, points however to a later date than 1490 when Prince Ferdinand of Capua conferred that title upon him.

Bibliography: S.M.M., 1955, pp. 122-123, n. 124; A. Bosero, 1975, p. 161.

Crivelli, Carlo
(from his workshop)

105a-d. *SS. Rocco, Sebastian, Emidio and the Blessed Jacopo della Marca*
Four panels, each 70 × 33 cm
(cat. n. 105)
Inscription: OPUS - CAROLUS - CRIVELLI - VENETI-, on panel of Jacopo della Marca
Acquisition: 1890, by purchase from the Pericoli family of Rome, who obtained these panels from the d'Aste collection in Genoa
Last restored: 1949

It is not known where the panels first came from. The inscription is generally agreed to be unreliable, though it could have been transcribed as a record of the original when the panels were removed from the group to which they belonged. The formal elements derive from the Crivelli *repertoire* but do not show the usual strongly felt tension which suggests that the secondary features of a larger work executed late in the artist's career were wholly entrusted to assistants. It is noted that San Rocco is portrayed in the dramatic rôle of a plague victim. The symptoms are typical: hollow eyes, cadaverous pallor and the plague swelling correctly detailed and located.

Bibliography: S.M.M., 1955, pp. 124-125, n. 125; A. Bosero, 1975, p. 102; G. Nepi Sciré, 1979, pp. 230-231.

Diana, Benedetto
see Rusconi, Benedetto

Diziani, Antonio
Venice 1737-1797

106. *Landscape with the Magdalene*
Oil on canvas, 133 × 118 cm
(cat. n. 455)
Acquisition: 1807, from the Old Academy of Venice

This is the canvas which Antonio, son of Gaspare Diziani, submitted with his request to be admitted to the Academy, which was granted on 11 September 1774.

Bibliography: S.M.M., 1970, p. 22 *et seq.*, n. 44.

Diziani, Gaspare

Belluno 1689 - Venice 1767

107. *Moses and the Burning Bush*
Oil on canvas, 56 × 96 cm
(cat. n. 459)
Acquisition: 1838, following the
suppression edicts

This and the picture which accompanies
it are considered to be works in which
Gaspare co-operated with his son Antonio, the father doing the figures and
the son the landscape.

Bibliography: S.M.M., 1970, p. 24, n.
49; A.P. Zugni Tauro, 1971, p. 93 et.
seq.

108. *Moses and the Tables of the Law*
Oil on canvas, 56 × 96 cm
(cat. n. 460)
Acquisition: 1838, following the
suppression edicts

Like the above, this picture shows indications of being a joint effort of Gaspare
and his son Antonio.

Bibliography: S.M.M., 1970, p. 24, n.
49; A.P. Zugni Tauro, 1971, p. 93 et
seq.

Fedeli, Domenico
(Maggiotto)

Venice 1713-1794

109. *Allegory of the Academy*
Oil on canvas, 130 × 92 cm
(cat. n. 443)
Acquisition: 1807, from the Old
Academy of Venice
Inscription: DOM^{CO} MAGGIOTTO F., in
lower right corner
Last restored: 1940

Probably donated to the Academy in
about 1763, the artist having been admitted in 1756. The work displays that
refined and academic type of over-
emphasis which Maggiotto brought to
popular styles of art decoration.

Bibliography: S.M.M., 1970, p. 52, n.
111.

Fetti, Domenico

Rome c. 1589 - Venice 1625

110. *David*
Oil on canvas, 175 × 128 cm
(cat. n. 669)
Acquisition: 1838, by gift of Girolamo
Contarini
Last restored: 1961

This striking picture dates from the years
that Fetti spent in Mantua where he was
able to admire works by Rubens and the
masterpieces of the great Venetian
painters of the Cinquecento. In Rome he
had already become familiar with Caravaggio's circle. With admirable freedom
the figure confidently adjusts to the light
and shade effects while displaying the
symbols of that day and age: the olive
green jacket with sleeves trimmed to the
fashionable length and a red feathered
cap worn in dashing style.

Bibliography: S.M.M., 1970, p. 25, n.
52.

111. *Meditation*
Oil on canvas, 179 × 140 cm
(cat. n. 671)
Acquisition: 1838, by gift of Girolamo
Contarini
Last restored: 1961

In this version of a theme which he
rendered in various forms, mostly dated
1616-1617 — there is one in the Louvre
in Paris — Fetti transforms the clearly
allegorical significance of the subject into highly detailed veracity with delightful
results.

Bibliography: S.M.M., 1970, p. 25 *et
seq.*, n. 53; R. Pallucchini, 1981, p. 137.

117

112. *A Girl reading*
Oil on canvas, 74 × 69 cm
(cat. n. 518)
Acquisition: 1838, by gift of Girolamo
Contarini
Last restored: 1961

This most successful portrayal of a girl
intent on reading is marked by the
realistic naturalness, delicacy and
preciosity through which Fetti so often
reveals his poetic qualities.

Bibliography: S.M.M., 1970, p. 24, n.
50.

113. *Parable of the Good Samaritan*
Oil on canvas, 61 × 45 cm
(cat. n. 503)
Acquisition: 1838, by gift of Girolamo
Contarini
Last restored: 1948

Among Fetti's most frequent subjects are
the parables. In this one of the Good
Samaritan painted in his Venetian period
between 1622 and 1625 he shows his
power of fantasy in all its creative
freshness.
Here the Gospel story is made the occasion of a natural scene of almost day-to-
day occurrence. Copies of the painting
are to be seen in the Boston Museum of
Fine Arts, in the Dresden Art Gallery and
in the Metropolitan Museum of Art in
New York.

Bibliography: S.M.M., 1970, p. 26, n.
54.

114. *Isaac amd Jacob*
Oil on canvas, 101 × 75 cm
(cat. n. 675)
Acquisition: 1838, by gift of Girolamo
Contarini

Previously thought to be a copy, this picture is in fact an authentic late work of
Fetti's, as shown by the flowing and expressive pictorial treatment of the subject.

Bibliography: S.M.M., 1970, p. 25, n.
51.

Fontebasso, Francesco
Venice 1709-1769

115. *The Adoration of the Magi*
Oil on canvas, 73 × 125 cm
(cat. n. 879)
Acquisition: 1924, by purchase from
the Trieste Export Office

This canvas, and the one accompanying it, were purchased as works by Sebastiano Ricci and were long attributed to him. Today they are in general rightly attributed to the youth of Francesco Fontebasso whose particular idiom is clearly recognisable. They were painted under the influence of Ricci in close brushwork and a sombre range of colours.

Bibliography: S.M.M., 1970, p. 29, n. 60.

116. *The Last Supper*
Oil on canvas, 75 × 125 cm
(cat. n. 880)
Acquisition: 1924, by purchase from
the Trieste Export Office

As in the case of the last picture, here Francesco Fontebasso again shows that he has the example of Sebastiano Ricci very much in mind.

Bibliography: S.M.M., 1970, p. 29, n. 71.

Galgario (Fra)
see Ghislandi, Vittore

Gaspari, Pietro
Venice 1720-1785

117. *Architectural Perspective*
Oil on canvas, 131 × 79 cm
(cat. n. 470)
Acquisition: 1807, from the Old
Academy of Venice
Inscription: PETRUS GASPARI/FA.^T
MDCCLXXV, at lower left
Last restored: 1859

This is the *"pièce de reception"* for Gaspari's election to the Academy. It demonstrates the aims and virtuosity of research practised by the so-called "perspective" movement of the Venetian Settecento, to which among lesser artists Antonio Visentini (see entry 308), Antonio Joli (see n. 135), Giuseppe Moretti (see n. 183) and Francesco Battaglioni (see n. 17) all belonged.

Bibliography: S.M.M., 1970, pp. 30-31, n. 64.

Ghislandi, Vittore
(Fra Galgario)
Bergamo 1655-1743

118. *Portrait of Count Giovanni
Battista Vailetti*
Oil on canvas, 226 × 137 cm
(cat. n. 778)
Acquisition: 1912, by purchase from
the Florence Export Office (A.
Olivotti)

Referred to in the collection of Countess Rosa Piatti Lochis, by the end of the Settecento this portrait was already known as one of Fra Galgario's most famous works. It dates from about 1710 when for some time the artist had been moving towards a clear preference for realistic attitudes of Lombard tradition. With dazzling brilliance Vailetti is shown in the privacy of his studio dressed in a resplendent costume. As well as the physical presence of the man, Ghislandi records the firm control he has of his feelings, and he does so with the rigour of an Illuminist.

Bibliography: S.M.M., 1970, p. 140, n. 31.

Giambono, Michele

Venetian - Records from 10
November 1420 to 20 April 1462

119. *The Coronation of the Virgin in Paradise among the angelic hierarchies, the saints, the four Doctors of the Church and the Evangelists*
Panel, 229 × 176 cm, with decoration in gilded plaster (cat. n. 33)
Inscription: IOANES ET ANTONIUS DE MURIANO F. / MCCCCXXXX, at lower centre with indistinct signature and date
Acquisition: 1816, by legacy of Girolamo Molin
Last restored: 1949

Most probably a work that was commissioned from Giambono for the Church of Sant'Agnese by Giovanni Dotto in 1447 for the price of 130 ducats. The condition was that it should be exactly similar to another that has been in the Church of San Pantalon since 1448 when it was painted by Antonio Vivarini and Giovanni d'Alemagna. The original cornice, ordered by Giambono from Francesco Moranzone, has been lost. The work, which may have been damaged by fire, was poorly repainted with a coating that was removed on restoration in 1949, but damage was confined to the upper zone from the scalloping as far as the last row of the saints. Although incomplete, this panel clearly shows that, in spite of restraints imposed by the client, the artist was able to introduce highly decorative and refined effects into the arrangement of the figures.

Bibliography: S.M.M., 1955, pp. 26-27, n. 24.

120. *Polyptych*
In central panel: *St. James the Greater*; in side panels, *St. John the Evangelist, Ven. Filippo Benizzi, the Archangel Michael and St. Louis of Toulouse*
Five panels, gold background engraved: central, 109 × 44 cm; lateral, each 88 × 29 cm (cat. n. 3)
Inscription: MICHAEL - ÇAMBONO PIXIT -, at foot of central panel
Acquisition: 1812, following the suppression edicts
Last restored: 1948

From the Scuola del Cristo at the Giudecca where it may originally have belonged to the Church of St. James on that island. The saint of that name is represented in the central compartment, as indicated on his staff and in the book opened at the passage in the Epistle of St. James (I, 22). On his left is Filippo Benizzi, founder of the Servites, without halo as he was not canonised until 1671, holding a Book of the Psalms open to the verse *"Servus tuus sum ego"*.
A late work of about 1450 in which, despite the sumptuously engraved gold backgrounds, the precious enamel-like colouring materials, the weary elegance reminiscent of Pisanello, these more forceful graphic elements relent slightly to suggest some knowledge, if not understanding, of Tuscan artists in

Venice, in particular Andrea del Castagno who was then working on his frescoes in the San Tarasio chapel in the Church of San Zaccaria. A study with variants resembling Filippo and St. Michael exists in the Albertina collection in Vienna.

Bibliography: S.M.M., 1955, pp. 27-28, n. 25; L. Magagnato, 1958, pp. 71-72; F. D'Arcais, 1976, p. 36.

*Gianfrancesco da Tolmezzo
see Žotti, Gianfrancesco*

Giolfino, Bartolomeo
Verona c. 1410 - c. 1486

121. *Polyptych*
At lower centre: *Madonna and Child on throne, between SS. Nicholas (?), John the Baptist, John the Evangelist and Francis;* in upper row, *The Coronation of the Virgin between SS. Georges, Peter, Jerome and Laurence (?);* on the pinnacles, in aedicules, *Two angels and Four bishops*
Carved wood, gilded and painted.
380 × 187 cm (cat. n. S.2)
Inscription: . . . ANCONA - A - FATOBARTOLA/MIO — ITA. . . / DI VERONA - 1740, enscrolled at base
Acquisition: 1909, by purchase from the heirs of Marchese A. Tacoli of Modena
Last restored: 1980

In 1905 this polyptych was on the antique market in Venice, having come from a private chapel of the Querinis at Pressana near Verona. In fact, the coat of arms of that family appears on the base, while the lilies of the same armorial bearings, which no longer display them, are woven as leaf-work on the painted socle. When last restored, additions which modified the iconography were removed even though this had the effect of showing up the loss of the original paintwork. A late work in which the features appear rather clumsy, but whose intaglios, though bitty, are of the finest workmanship in the Gothic tradition.

Bibliography: S.M.M., 1955, pp. 189-190, n. 212.

Giordano, Luca
Naples 1634-1705

122. *The Crucifixion of St. Peter*
Oil on canvas, 196 × 258 cm
(cat. n. 751)
Inscription: L. GIORDANO T., 1692, written in a later hand at lower right
Acquisition: 1910, by purchase from the Venice Export Office
Last restored: 1984

The date of this painting, of which there is a replica in the Church of San Francesco Saverio in Paris, is generally put at the end of the sixth decade of the 17th century. Recent restoration shows, however, that any influence that Ribera might earlier have had loses ground here to the easy-flowing style of the artist, and this suggests a much later date for this work. Similar examples in which the colour seems to be melting away in a process of slow combustion were fundamental to the renewal of painting in Venice with the approach of the Settecento.

Bibliography: S.M.M., 1970, p. 142, n. 314.

Giorgione
Castelfranco 1476/77 - Venice 1510

123. *The Storm*
Oil on canvas, 68 × 59 cm
(cat. n. 915)
Inscription: the Carraresi coat of arms on the right of the tower
Acquisition: 1932, by purchase from the heirs of Prince Giovanelli
Last restored: 1984

The picture was commissioned from Giorgione by Gabriele Vendramin in whose house it was noted by Marcantonio Michiel in 1530, and in all likelihood it remained in this family until the end of the Settecento. In the mid-19th century it was mentioned as being in the Manfrin collection. Then, in 1875, it was chosen for the Berlin Museum but was declared unfit for trans-

port and was purchased by Prince Giovanelli.
Many different modern interpretations have been conjured up as to the subject of this small canvas, the meaning of which was unintelligible even to contemporaries if Michiel's reference to "the little town with the storm, the *cingana* and the soldier" is accepted. In one early version Giorgione devised and completed a female nude at the water's edge in the place of the soldier with the long staff. Moreover, recent reflectoscopic examinations have brought to light another design for the town in the background. This strengthens the view of those who think that the picture grew out of a fantasy without subject and merely reflects the artist's state of mind at the time. On the other hand, many figurative parallels be-

tween *The Storm* and certain passages in *Hypnerotomachia Poliphili*, which was published in 1499, can be adduced. The above helps to explain why it was that this famous picture came to be painted at the turn of the 15th century in a refined humanistic age when "hidden subjects" were greatly admired, at least by the initiated few. The enigma behind it increases the fascination of this small canvas in which Giorgione, at the end of his first working decade, enters that definitive period which led the way for painting in its modern form. Free from any sort of tie with design or perspective, colour was now to create the painter's imagery in a new spatial and environmental fusion. And so, in the very moment when a flash of lightning opens the rain clouds, we see two beings lost in thought; we see ancient ruins, houses shrouded in greenery ringing the colour changes with distant shades of blue and grey, with the lazy movement of a stream, the emerald-green of a meadow and a tree-lined gorge. A moment of consternation is suggested in the highly coloured notes that are struck by a succession of blends and glazes in which the Giorgionesque concept slowly gives new reality to pictorial art.

Bibliography: S.M.M., 1962, p. 119 *et seq.*, n. 198; Id., 1978, p. 99 *et. seq.*; T. Pignatti, 1978, p. 104 n. 14; G. Nepi Sciré, 1985.

121

124. *The Old Woman*
Oil on canvas, 68 × 59 cm
(cat. n. 272)
Inscription: COL TEMPO, on scroll in the subject's right hand
Acquisition: 1856, by purchase from the Manfrin collection
Last restored: 1984

Together with *The Storm*, was once in the collection of Gabriele Vendramin where this "portrait of the mother of Zorzon by the hand of Zorzon" in its present frame was recorded for the first time in 1569. It then passed into the Manfrin collection. After various erroneous attributions (Torbido, Cariani, Tiziano) it is today almost unanimously accepted as a work of Giorgione dating from towards the end of the first decade of the Cinquecento. In its realism it seems to reflect a momentary pause on Giorgione's part to meditate not so much on Dürer's actual works as on the vigorous new ideas that were being actively pursued in those years by his great follower, Tiziano Vecellio. The picture has been given many interpretations, but all are based on different readings of the inscription *Col Tempo* and to its allusion to the passing of time and to fading beauty. Here that unwelcome reality is expressed by the artist in the purest of terms obtained by light and the way it graduates with unerring accuracy the most subtle tones of colour.

Bibliography: S.M.M., 1962, p. 124, n. 199; T. Pignatti, 1978, p. 144 *et seq.*; C. Nepi Sciré, 1985.

Giovanni Agostino da Lodi
(Pseudo-Boccaccino)

active between the late 1400s and the early 1500s

125. *Christ washing the Apostles' feet*
Panel, 132 × 111 cm (cat. n. 509)
Inscription: MCCCCC, on seat at left
Acquisition: 1856, by purchase from the Manfrin collection
Last restored: 1979

Until 1875 this picture was listed in the catalogue of Manfrin's collection as the work of Perugino. It was subsequently attributed to Boccaccino and from then on to Pseudo-Boccaccino, whom current historiography also identifies with Agostino delle Prospettive who was working in about 1508 in Bologna as the Giovanni Agostino da Lodi known to be in Venice in 1504. The work is regarded as one of the key paintings of Venetian art in the last decade of the 1400s and the first years of the 16th century. It is notable for the use of figures similar to those of Leonardo and Bramante, which aspect has never been fully discussed. However, the close link with these two great artists was soon to be recognised and imitated in Venetian circles.

Bibliography: S.M.M., 1955, pp. 169-170, n. 189; D. Gioseffi, 1978, pp. 97-98.

Giovanni da Bologna
records from 1377 to 1389

126. *The Madonna of Humility, with angels of the Annunciation, the Confraternity of the School of St. John the Evangelist, the Baptist and SS. Peter, John the Evangelist and Paul*
Panel, 110 × 97 cm (cat. n. 17)
Inscription: ÇVANE. DA. BOLOGNA. PENSE., at centre of base
Acquisition: 1812, following the suppression edicts
Last restored: 1948

Originally in the *albergo* of the School of St. John the Evangelist, whose symbol is seen in the banner which one of the brothers is holding, this is a work of rare brilliance. The Bolognese painter signs himself here in the Venetian style, Giovanni becoming Zuane, a sign that he has fully adapted himself to artistic life on the lagoons; another is his adherence to the Gothicism of Lorenzo Veneziano. For this reason, and because it appears to be an earlier work than his St. Christopher of 1377, which is in Padua Museum, the panel can be ascribed to the first years of the eighth decade of the 14th century.

Bibliography: S.M.M., 1955, pp. 8-9, n. 5; R. Pallucchini, 1964, p. 186.

Giovanni d'Alemagna
see Vivarini, Antonio and Giovanni D'Alemagna

Girolamo da Treviso il Vecchio
(Aviano, Girolamo)
records from 1476 - Treviso 1497

127. *The Transfiguration*
Panel in the form of a lunette, 172 × 263 cm (cat. n. 96)
Acquisition: 1812, following the suppression edicts

From the Church of Santa Margherita in Treviso, where its place was over an altar erected at the behest of Vittore da Norcia and bearing the date of 1488, this lunette must have formed the upper part of a lost altarpiece referred to in sources as a *Transfiguration*. Traditional attribution was to this problematical artist, now identified with Girolamo Aviano — a Girolamo da Treviso was also working there at that time — is now regarded as a convincing one, being supported by comparison with his known works and, more directly by his practice of painting in a succession of neat close segments.

Bibliography: S.M.M., 1955, pp. 130-131, n. 134; G. Nepi Sciré, 1973, p. 30.

128. *Madonna Enthroned between a Franciscan Bishop and SS. Anthony, Francis and Prosdocimo (or Basil)*
Panel, 210 × 214 cm (cat. n. 886)
Inscription: HIERONIMUS / TARVISIO - P - MCCCC LXXXXIIII, on step of throne
Acquisition: 1918, by sequestration of enemy property after the First World War
Last restored: 1963

Originally in the Chapel of the Cross in the Castle of Collalto, or in the Church of San Giovanni, this late work of Girolamo da Treviso is the last of his to be dated. In style it is not unlike an altarpiece that was once in San Vigilio di Montebelluna and is now in the sacristy of the Cathedral Canons in Treviso. Worked with "antonellesque" lucidity the various figurative elements make up a most harmonious whole.

Bibliography: S.M.M., 1955, p. 131, n. 135; G. Nepi Sciré, 1973, p. 32.

Guardi, Francesco
Venice 1712-1793

129. *St. Mark's Basin with St. George's and the Giudecca*
Oil on canvas, 72 × 97 cm
(cat. n. 709)
Inscription: F.G., on a box in boat in foreground
Acquisition: 1903, by gift of the Prince Regent of Liechtenstein

In this late version of one of Francesco Guardi's favourite views the artist re-states a wish to record the true ap-pearance of the scene in fleeting colours which are both evocative and charmingly allusive. His is a method that is far from the incomparably poetic objectivity of Canaletto.

Bibliography: S.M.M., 1970, pp. 33-34, n. 69; A. Morassi, 1973, p. 391, n. 427.

130. *The Island of Anconetta*
Oil on canvas, 34 × 53 cm
(cat. n. 706)
Acquisition: 1903, by gift of M. Guggenheim
Last restored: 1983

This veduta — one of the last that Guardi painted — originally came from the Mairi collection in Padua, and there is a preliminary drawing for it in the Metropolitan Museum of Art in New York. Its very recent restoration has brought to light a liveliness of touch which had hitherto been obscured by heavy repainting intended to check the flaking of the colours.

Bibliography: S.M.M., 1970, p. 34, n. 70; A. Morassi, 1973, p. 433, n. 600.

131. *Fire at the San Marcuola oil deposit*
Oil on canvas, 41 × 60 cm
(cat. n. 1344)
Acquisition: 1971, by purchase from the Milan Export Office

When Francesco Guardi set out to record unusual events in the city, like the disastrous fire that swept through the San Marcuola oil deposit in December 1789, he did not abandon his poetic urge to present the reality of the scene in highly allusive imagery. He would first docu-ment it with graphic, lifelike drawings made on the spot. There is a preliminary drawing for this picture in the Metropolitan Museum of Art in New York.

Bibliography: A. Morassi, 1973, pp. 206, 369, n. 312.

Jacobello del Fiore
records from 1400 - d. between 20 October and 8 November 1439

132. *The Madonna of the Misericordia between SS. John the Baptist and John the Evangelist*
Panel, gold background, 86 × 113 cm, with adornments in gilded plaster
(cat. n. 13)
Inscription: 1436 IACHOMÈLLO DE FLOR PENSE, not original
Acquisition: 1816, by legacy of Girolamo Molin
Last restored: 1951

The provenance of the panel is unknown. The date and signature are spurious, though they could have been copied from a former inscription on the original frame. In any case, the transcribed date is er-roneous, nor does it correspond with the character of the work. With the elimina-tion of the 19th century surround, fragments of painting unaffected by light or subsequent coatings emerged along the lower edges. Although the iconographic concept of the Platytera Madonna and Misericordia together may have been taken from Paolo Veneziano (see entry 197), the painting shows the influence of Gentile da Fabriano and is a varia-tion of a subject already tried out in 1407 in his *Montegranaro Triptych* now in a private collection in Switzerland. Compared with the latter it shows a more skilled and subtle elegance, less iconic rigidity; there is too a real attempt to characterise the small kneeling figures. It probably dates between 1415 and 1420.

Bibliography: S.M.M., 1955, p. 29, n. 27; C. Huter, 1978, p. 36.

133. *Triptych*
In central panel, *Justice*; in side panels, *SS. Michael and Gabriel*
Three panels, central 208×194 cm; *St. Michael* part panel on left, 208×133 cm; *St. Gabriel*, 208×163 cm; adornments in gilded plaster (cat. n. 15)
Inscription: IACOBELLUS DE/FLORE PINXIT 1421, to left of *Justice* over the lion
Acquisition: 1884
Last restored: 1946

The signature and date are not the original ones but correspond closely to source indications. The upper cornice is in part remade and regilded, while some repainting, with alterations, has been noted, especially at the centre. The iconographic source nearest to St. Michael, who is in the act of killing the dragon, is a mosaic in the Baptistery in St. Mark's. In the Latin of the scrolls, Gabriel, the announcing angel, pleads

with the Virgin to act with humanity in the dark world of man, while Michael, angel of peace, begs her to distribute awards and punishments according to merit. Behind the figure of Justice the enscrolled couplet reads: "I will carry out the warnings of the angels and the Holy Scriptures and be gentle to the pious, the enemy of evildoers, and disdainful of the proud"; words which are generally ascribed in nordic art to Christ the Judge. It is clear that Justice is identified here with Venice, as shown in an almost contemporary relief on the west façade of the Ducal Palace in this case complicated by linking Venice, Justice and Peace with the Virgin Mary, Justice and Peace being concepts fundamental to Venetian ideology. An important official commission for the artist, in its complex symbology this work fully accords with the courtly Gothic style. That style, interpreted with appropriate decorativeness, as with coeval architecture and sculpture, may be said to be "flowery".

Bibliography: S.M.M., 1955, pp. 28-29, n. 26; S. Sinding-Larsen, 1974, pp. 55-56; B. Degenhart - A. Schmitt, 1980, pp. 140-141, 153.

Jacobello del Fiore
(and assistants)

134. *Coronation of the Virgin in Paradise among the Evangelists, angelic hierarchies, patriarchs, prophets, martyrs, saints and virgins*
Panel, 283×303 cm, adorned with plaster and gilded stucco (cat. n. 1)
Inscription: band at centre of throne is inscribed with verses taken from Guariento's *Paradise* frescoes in the Great Council Hall of the Doge's Palace
Acquisition: 1882, by purchase from the Cathedral of Ceneda
Last restored: 1948

In a poor state of preservation with the paint layers worn and eroded and in several places the adornments gone. Originally commissioned for the high altar in Ceneda Cathedral by Antonio Correr, Bishop of that city from 1410 to 1445, who is thought to be the kneeling figure towards the right at base. The date and signature enscrolled at the foot of the throne are believed to have been cancelled during restoration in 1840. According to

Caffi, who in 1880 passed on an oral tradition, they were as follows: "Iac. de. flore p. 1438." On the original frame, which Caffi read directly, was the inscription: "Christofalo da Ferrara engraved (*intajo*) 1438 on 10 February." This work, which is an abridged and horizontally compressed version of Guariento's *Paradise*, has recently been attributed to an unknown artist called "Maestro di Ceneda". None the less, despite its tired, repetitious style, it is attributed to Jacobello and his assistants and the retouching to Jacobello himself.

Bibliography: S.M.M., 1955, pp. 30-31, n. 28; C. Huter, 1973, p. 33; M. Muraro, 1975, pp. 73-74.

Jacopo da Montagnana
see Parisati, Jacopo

Joli, Antonio
Modena c. 1700 - Naples 1777

135. *Perspective of ancient Baths*
Oil on canvas, 130 × 93 cm
(cat. n. 450)
Acquisition: 1807, from the Old
Academy of Venice
Last restored: 1859

The artist's "pièce de réception" when
joining the Academy of Venice to which
he was elected as a member at the ses-
sion of 13 February 1756. It is a typical
example of the painting of this Modenese
artist who, after working as a scenery
designer until shortly before 1740, went
to Venice where he became one of the
foremost exponents of the "perspective"
genre in which he was later to win much
success in Germany, in London and
Madrid.

Bibliography: S.M.M., 1970, p. 36, n.
74.

Lama, Giulia
Venice 1681-1747

136. *Judith and Holofernes*
Oil on canvas, 107 × 155 cm
(cat. n. 1345)
Acquisition: 1976, by purchase from
Milan Export Office

In this biblical subject painted in about
1730 Giulia Lama shows how well able
she was to apply the harsh colouring and
chiaroscuro effects of Giambattista
Piazzetta to a highly charged situation
of melodramatic intensity. The theatrical
setting and use of light are most skilfully
combined and evaluated.

Bibliography: U. Ruggeri, 1983, p. 124.

Licinio, Bernardino
Poscante c. 1490 - Venice c. 1565

137. *Portrait of a Lady with "il
balzo" Hair-style*
Oil on canvas, 48 × 46 cm
(cat. n. 305)
Acquisition: 1838, by gift of Girolamo
Contarini

Once said to be by Pordenone, or after
him, this portrait is now securely attributed to Bernardino Licinio. It is in
warm colours and speaks of a sweet and
intimate disposition.

Bibliography: S.M.M., 1962, p. 129, n.
205; L. Vertova, 1975, p. 305.

138. *Portrait of a Lady*
Oil on canvas, 76 × 60 cm
(cat n. 303)

Inscription: E.A. XLVIII / A.A.XV, beneath two coats of arms perhaps of the Morello family of Treviso

Acquisition: 1850, by legacy of Felicita Renier

Previously ascribed to Paris Bordone but now considered with certainty to be by Licinio, who was already in Venice by 1511 working as a follower first of Giorgione and later of Palma il Vecchio. However, this portrait, painted in the 1540s, does indeed show the influence of Paris Bordone in the way it strives after colour and figural effects.

Bibliography: S.M.M., 1962, p. 129, n. 204.

Liss, Johann
Odelburg im Holstein cv. 1597 -
Venice 1629

139. *Apollo and Marsyas*
Oil on canvas, 58 × 48 cm

Acquisition: 1838, by gift of Girolamo Contarini

The painting of Johann Liss owes much of its early formation to his stay in Rome among the Dutch admirers of Caravaggio. This he enriched with Venetian experience, the two influences combining here in a bloodthirsty subject depicting the flaying of Marsyas which the painter treats with deeply felt emphasis amounting to glee.

Bibliography: S.M.M., 1970, p. 42, n. 88; Johann Liss, 1975, p. 95 *et seq.*, n. A 24.

140. *Abel mourned by his parents*
Oil on canvas, 67.5 × 89 cm
(cat. n. 913)

Acquisition: 1932, by purchase from the Giovanelli collection, Venice
Last restored: 1959

To his parents' melancholy contemplation of the lifeless body of Abel, Liss matches a sad and desolate countryside bathed in the light of a sunset washed by blending tones of gold and red.

Bibliography: S.M.M., 1970, p. 42, n. 89; Johann Liss, 1975, p. 120 *et seq.*; R. Pallucchini, 1981, p. 146.

141. *The Sacrifice of Isaac*
Oil on canvas, 66 × 85 cm
(cat. n. 914)

Acquisition: 1932, by purchase from the Giovanelli collection, Venice
Last restored: 1959

Like its companion picture above, this canvas is ascribed to the Venetian years of the artist (1624-1629). Liss painted other versions of the same subject in varying form, the best of which are now in the Uffizi in Florence and the Bredins Museum at the Hague. More markedly than in his other works in these Galleries the artist extends the dramatic impact of the event horizontally into the operatic background of a widening landscape.

Bibliography: S.M.M., 1970, pp. 90-91.

Longhi, Alessandro
Venice 1733-1813

142. *The Family of the Procurator Luigi Pisani*
Oil on canvas, 255 × 341 cm
(cat. n. 1355)
Inscription: LONGHJ on global map; on upper border of the pages of the book at corner on right is the original fragmentary signature: ALESSANDRO ABATE; below to the right is the added apocryphal signature OPUS PIETRO LONGHI, father of Alessandro
Acquisition: 1979, by purchase from the Agostino Nani Mocenigo collection, Venice
Last restored: 1959

This is one of the two great portraits executed by Alessandro Longhi in 1758 for the family of Pisani of Santo Stefano. The first, a fragment of which is still in the Museo Civico at Belluno, was of the family of Ermolao Alvise I Andrea Pisani while this one portrays Procurator Luigi Pisani (1701- 1767) with his wife Paolina Gambara, his sons and daughters Ermolao I Alvise, Elena, Ermolao II Carlo, Elisabetta, his father the Doge Alvise Pisani, brothers Ermolao IV Giovanni Francesco and Ermolao II Francesco, perhaps also the Abbot Don Giovanni Gregorietti. A vast painting, and certainly one of the great masterpieces of European portraiture of the Settecento, in it Alessandro Longhi gives a grown-up dimension to the small figures that his father Pietro had painted before him. He does so without losing any of their colourful appearance, grouping them all into a splendid setting which seems to anticipate Goya.

Bibliography: F. Valcanover, 1961, p. 229; T. Pignatti, 1968. p. 139.

143. *Painting and Merit*
Oil on canvas, 128 × 93 cm
(cat. n 493)
Inscription: ALESSAND / LONGHI / PINX, on back of volume supported by hand
Acquisition: 1807, from the Old Academy of Venice
Last restored: 1958

While this allegorical subject was required of the artist for his election to membership of the Academy in 1759, its stylistic character is more in keeping with his work towards the end of the 1770s. Longhi made an engraving of the picture and dedicated it to John Udry, English Consul in Venice in 1761 and again from 1773 to 1775.

Bibliography: S.M.M., 1970, p. 44, n. 93.

144. *Portrait of Carlo Lodoli*
Oil on canvas, 127 × 93 cm
(cat. n. 908)
Inscription: FRATER LODOLI / IN APOLOGIS. CONSCRIBENDIS. ET IN ARCHITECTONICA. / HAUD INTER SUPREMUS ANNUMERANDUS. / ALEXANDER LONGHI PINXIT, top left
Acquisition: 1930, by gift of Count A. di Robilant
Last restored: 1958-1959

This portrait of a date just prior to 1770 is an exemplary one for its spontaneous and revealing presentation of the stern character of a famous authority on architecture and merciless critic of his contemporaries in that profession. X-ray examination has shown that beneath the picture there is another of a young nobleman wearing a wig.

Bibliography: S.M.M., 1970, p. 45, n. 94.

128

145. *The Concert*
Oil on canvas, 60 × 48 cm
(cat. n. 466)
Inscription: PETRUS LONGHI 1741, on back of picture
Acquisition: 1838, by gift of Girolamo Contarini
Last restored: 1955

The first costume painting to be dated and signed by Pietro Longhi who, having given up working on historic scenes, went to Bologna and studied under Giuseppe Maria Crespi. Then, from the 1730s on, he devoted himself to portraying the social life of his days with kindly irony but without ignoring the least sign of colour or the most exiguous of emotions characteristic of that age. With matchless charm he shows here the zeal of the three musicians and the indifference of the listeners who are more interested in their game of cards.

Bibliography: S.M.M., 1970, p. 47 *et seq.*, n. 99.

146. *The Tailor*
Oil on canvas, 60 × 49 cm
(cat. n. 469)
Acquisition: 1838, by gift of Girolamo Contarini
Last restored: 1955

While avoiding any attempt to moralise, Pietro Longhi applied his subtle irony to describing in tender shades of colour the moments, even trivial ones, in the daily lives of his contemporaries. This one of examining dress materials also dates from 1741 judging the similarity of its style to that of *The Concert*.

Bibliography: S.M.M., 1970, p. 48, n. 102.

147. *The Dancing Lesson*
Oil on canvas, 60 × 49 cm
(cat. n. 465)
Acquisition: 1838, by gift of Girolamo Contarini
Last restored: 1955

Pietro portrays what was one of the most time-absorbing activities of the ladies of Venice, dancing, and with customary accuracy he extracts from the scene every detail of colour.

Bibliography: S.M.M., 1970, p. 48, n. 100.

148. *La Toilette*
Oil on canvas, 60 × 49 cm
(cat. n. 464)
Acquisition: 1838, by gift of Girolamo Contarini
Last restored: 1955

Under the indifferent gaze of the elderly domestic and the servile attitudes affected by the two assistants the dressing of a lady of fashion is completed.

Bibliography: S.M.M., 1970, p. 48, n. 101.

149. *The Fortune Teller*
Oil on canvas, 60 × 49 cm
(cat. n. 468)
Inscription: PIETRO LONGHI, on back of picture
Acquisition: 1838, by gift of Girolamo Contarini
Last restored: 1955

Rarely did Pietro Longhi treat subjects touching the life of the populace. Yet when he did enter into the daily existence of humble folk he knew how to portray familiar customs with his usual skill in capturing physical and mental attitudes. This little scene takes place beneath the porticoes of the Ducal Palace and dates from 1752.

Bibliography: S.M.M., 1970, p. 49, n. 103.

150. *The Pharmacist*
Oil on canvas, 60 × 48 cm
(cat. n. 467)
Inscription: PIETRO LONGHI, on back of picture
Acquisition: 1838, by gift of Girolamo Contarini
Last restored: 1955

An extremely evocative picture of the interior of an 18th century chemist's shop in Venice painted by Longhi in 1752. In the depths of the shop furnishings and shelves of jars speak of the wear and tear of daily use. And the figures in their muffled silence seem fixed in dumbstruck stillness, recalling forever a completely lost age.

Bibliography: S.M.M., 1970, p. 49, n. 104.

Lorenzo Veneziano
active from 1356 to 1372

151. *Polyptych*
Lower row, central compartment:
The Annunciation; lateral
compartments, left: *SS. Anthony
Abbot, John the Baptist, Paul and
Peter*; lateral compartments, right: *SS.
John the Evangelist and the
Magdalene, Dominic and Francis.*
Upper row, eight half figures of
Prophets, with *The Eternal Father
giving the Blessing* in central
compartment; lateral compartments:
in the predella five quatrefoils with
busts of hermit saints, from left:
*Saba, Macarius, Paul, Hilary and
Theodore.* In the pilasters dividing the
compartments: thirty-six small figures
of saints whose names are written to
the side of each. Known also as the
Lion Polyptych, the work contains
two rows of panels with gold backgrounds: central compartment, lower,
126 × 75 cm; four lateral
compartments, each, 121 × 60 cm;
upper central compartment, adapted,
82 × 83 cm; eight lateral
compartments, each 67 × 30 cm;
thirty-six small panels in the pilasters,
each 35 × 5 cm (cat. n. 10)
Inscription: MCCCLVII/HEC/TABELLA/FCA

FUIT 7...C (FCA FUIT & HIC) / AFFISSA P̄ /
LAURĒ CIUS / PICTORES / 7 ÇANINUS
SC/ULTORES ITPE / REGIS VEN VI/RI DNI
FRIS/ÇOTI/D̄ ABBA/TIB·D̄ FLOT P̄/OIS 7 FU....
(IOIS & FUNTO/MON... TI/MONIS ISTI) / HANC
TUIS /. . . S AGNE / TRIUNPHATO / ORBIS. . .
/ DOMINICUS / LION EGO / NUNC
SUPPLEX(NUNC SUPPLX) / ARTE PRE /
POLITAM / DONO TA/BELLAM, on two
revised plaques on either side of the
central panel of the predella. In
addition, on the left side of the step
of the throne in the central
compartment is the date MCCCLVIII
Acquisition: 1812, following the
suppression edicts

Originally in the destroyed Church of
Sant'Antonio di Castello (see entry n. 81),
this polyptych was commissioned for 300
ducats by Domenico Lion, a co-opted
member of the Senate for 1367-1368,
who had himself portrayed as the small
figure kneeling at the Virgin's feet in the
central compartment. As well as giving
the date when the work was begun,
1357, the inscription names the artist as
Lorenzo, the carver of the cornices as
Zanino, the founder of the church, Giotto
degli Abati, and lastly the identity of the

donor. While being moved in the 19th
century the polyptych was taken apart
and damaged. It was then that one of
the central panels was lost and the present *Father Eternal* was painted in replace-
ment, probably by Diana. Nor are the
ten small figures of saints on the pilasters
original. They were probably re-done
during the same restoration, as also was
the framework which has nevertheless
preserved the whole structure in its
original form. Executed, as it was, between 1357 and 1359, the work shows
some Byzantine elements derived from
Paolo Veneziano, but it is marked by a
beautifully elegant Gothic style most
notable in the figures of the saints. The
Annunciation deviates from the solemn
and frontal encounter of tradition to
benefit by a naturalistic treatment derived
perhaps from contemporary Bolognese
art. Contrasts between these two schools
is blunted by rich chromatic effects which
draw on a wide range of colours. Beneath
the framework — and perhaps not by
mere chance — are brushwork tests in
pure colour and some quickly sketched
carbon drawings still of fresh appearance.
Bibliography: S.M.M., 1955, pp. 9-11,
n. 6; R. Pallucchini, 1964, pp. 167-170.

152. *The Marriage of St. Catherine*
Panel, gold background, 95 × 58 cm
(cat. n. 650)
Inscription: M.CCC.LVIIII.AD.XX...D̄
FEVRARO FO FATA/Sᵗᵃ ANCONA P MAN DE
LOREÇO PENTOR·: IN VENEXIA., at base
Acquisition: 1900, by gift of the
Udine Seminary
Last restored: 1948

The original location of this work is not
known, but it is believed to have been
central to a polyptych. Once in the Manin
family in Venice, then bought by Jacopo
Danieli from whom it passed to Count
Pellegrini of Zara and then into the Cernazai collection, it finally came to rest
in the Seminary at Udine. Signed and

dated 2 February 1359, Venetian calen-
dar and therefore in 1360, it clearly
shows that Lorenzo sought here to get
away from the Byzantine tradition to
which the large mandorla, or almond-
shaped background of Gothic origins, is
adapted. In the lively movement of the
Child, the delicate elegance of the saint
and angels and the soft chromatic effects
are seen the influence of Vitale of Bologna
and Tommaso of Modena.

Bibliography: S.M.M., 1955, pp. 11-12,
n. 7; R. Pallucchini, 1964, p. 170.

153. *Polyptych*
In central panel: *The Annunciation*;
in side panels: *SS. Gregory, the
Baptist, James and Stephen*
Five panels, gold background, central
111 × 54 cm; lateral, each 94 × 24
cm (cat. n. 9)

Inscription: MCCC. LXXI. LAURECI. PINSIT.,
at foot of central panel on step of
throne
Acquisition: 1816, by legacy of
Girolamo Molin

Last restored: 1949

The original whereabouts of this work,
which has lost much of its background
gilding, is unknown. Despite a certain
heaviness in the figures of the Virgin and
the angel in particular, a sensitive use of
light and of rich decorative colours for
the lateral saints is very striking. But the
novelty of this painting lies in the introduction of a flower besprinkled ground,
perhaps one of the first examples of its

kind. This trend was to be fully developed by international taste for the Gothic
style already foreshadowed in panels now
in the Berlin Museum.

Bibliography: S.M.M., 1955, p. 13, n.
9; R. Pallucchini, 1964, p. 176.

154a,b. *St. Peter and St. Mark*
Two panels, gold background, each
114 × 44 cm (cat. ns. 5, 5a)

Inscription: MCCC. LXXXI. MESE NOVEB.
at foot of St. Peter panel; LAURECI.
PINXIT. HOC. OP., at foot of St. Mark
panel

Acquisition: 1812, following the
suppression edicts

Last restored: 1948

Originally in the Silk Office at the Rialto
where they formed a unique group with
a *Resurrection of Christ*, now in the
Museo Civico of Milan, and a *Madonna*
which was perhaps similar to the *Madonna of the Rose* of the Kress Foundation
in Birmingham Museum, Alabama.
Comparison of these panels with the *Annunciation* of the same date, 1371 (see
153 above), shows that a new solemni-
ty and a more profound taste for formal-
ity had entered into the characterisation
of the two saints.

Bibliography: S.M.M., 1955, pp. 12-13,
n. 8; R. Pallucchini, 1964, pp 176-177.

Lotto, Lorenzo
Venice c. 1480 - Loreto 1556

155. *Portrait of a young gentleman
in his study*
Oil on canvas, 98 × 111 cm
(cat. n. 912)

Acquisition: 1930, by purchase from
Count Eduardo Rovero di Treviso

Last restored: 1982

Dating from about 1528, this is certainly one of the best known and most
fascinating pieces of portraiture to come
from the brush of Lorenzo Lotto. With
it he attains a supreme moment in his
alert and questing sensitivity. The young
nobleman, a lover of hunting and music,
is caught during a pause in his reading
to meditate on some obscure and absorb-
ing thought. The cold light that enters
from the window at the left illuminates

with unexpected subtlety the grey and
black of his clothes, the pinkish-white
flesh, the greens, light blues, pinks and
whites of the disorderly ordered still life
on the table.

Bibliography: S.M.M., 1962, p. 131, n.
209; G. Mariani Canova, 1975, p. 110;
L. Puppi, 1980, p. 398; P. Zampetti,
1983, plate 32.

Luciani, Sebastiano
(Sebastiano del Piombo)
(attributed to)

156. *Sacred Conversation*
Tempera on panel, 50 × 81 cm
(cat. n. 70)
Acquisition: 1838, by gift of Girolamo
Contarini

Variously attributed to Previtali, to
Cariani, Licinio, Palma il Vecchio,
Catena, and to Giorgione himself as a
work of about 1505, the general view
now is that this is one of the first pictures
to be painted by Sebastiano del Piom-

bo when he was still hesitating between
the teaching of Giovanni Bellini and acceptance of what was then the modern
style of Giorgione.

Bibliography: S.M.M., 1962, p. 126, n.
201; E. Merkel, 1978, p. 96; T. Pignatti,
1978, p. 139, n. A.56; M. Hirst, 1981,
pp. 4, 5, 26, 94.

Maffei, Francesco
Vicenza c. 1600 - Padua 1660

157. *Perseus beheads Medusa*
Oil on canvas, 130 × 160 cm
(cat. n. 1340)
Acquisition: 1968, by purchase from
Katherine L. Gonusz of Miami
Beach, Florida
Last restored: 1968

This picture and its companion (see 158
below), which date from the late 1650s,
were in Budapest until the early years of
this century. They are both highly imaginative works by the independent and
gifted Vicenza artist, Francesco Maffei,
whose painting developed along baroque
lines set by Fetti, Liss and Strozzi.

Bibliography: S.M.M., 1970, p. 239, n.
586; R. Pallucchini, 1981, p. 192.

158. *Mythological scene*
Oil on canvas, 130 × 160 cm
(cat. n. 1341)
Acquisition: 1968, by purchase from
Katherine L. Gonusz of Miami
Beach, Florida
Last restored: 1968

As in the picture above, the figures seem
to step from any attachment to the canvas into a sort of theatrical and dreamy
distortion of physical and spiritual attitudes which has the effect of stressing
the formal values of the artist's style.

Bibliography: S.M.M., 1970, p. 239, n.
587; R. Pallucchini, 1981, p. 192.

Maggiotto, Domenico
see Fedeli, Domenico

Maggiotto, Francesco
Venice 1750-1805

159. *Allegory of Painting*
Oil on canvas, 130 × 115 cm
(cat. n. 442)

Inscription: FRANCO MAGGIOTTO, on folio near palette on right

Acquisition: 1807, from the Old Academy of Venice

Executed in 1769, this is the artist's set piece for his election to the Academy in the previous year. While the female figure allegorises Painting, the one half-standing beside her represents Nature. The youth on the right is evidently symbolic of Design. This allegory is extremely indicative of the retrogression of Venetian painting in the second half of the 18th century towards an affected and mannered style brought on by the spread of neo-classical ideas.

Magnasco, Alessandro
Genoa 1667-1749

160. *Christ adored by two nuns*
Oil on canvas, 58 × 43 cm
(cat. n. 909)

Acquisition: 1929, by gift of Benno Geiger

The almost casual brushwork and contrasting light effects of Alessandro Magnasco, so well represented in this little picture, strongly recall the work of other Venetian painters at the beginning of the 18th century, especially Sebastiano and Mario Ricci.

Bibliography: S.M.M., 1970, p.143, n.316.

Mansueti, Giovanni
records from 1485 - 1527

161. *Miracle of the Relic of the Holy Cross in the Campo San Lio*
Oil on canvas, 318 × 458 cm
(cat. n. 564)

Inscription: OPUS / IOANNIS D / MANSUETI/S VENETI / RECTE SE/NTIENTIUM BELLI/NI DISCIPLI, on card held by figure on left

Acquisition: 1820, following the suppression edicts

Last restored: 1958-1960

Once in the Sala dell'Albergo or della Croce at the School of St. John the Evangelist (see n. 16), this and the picture below (see n. 162) formed part of the Miracles of the Cross series. The large canvas tells of a miraculous event which occurred in 1474 during the funeral of one of the brothers who had little respect

for the relic. As a result the relic became so heavy that it had to be substituted and passed into the care of the priest of San Lio. The *Opuscolo dei Miracoli* (1590) states that the picture was painted in 1494. Mansueti, who may have intended the figure on the left holding a paper scroll to be a portrayal of himself, almost certainly used for this picture part of a preliminary drawing by Gentile Bellini which is in the Uffizi Gallery.
The urban scene is rather naïvely handled and, in a passive sense, owes something to Bellini and to a lesser extent Carpaccio. On the extreme right there is a curious notice on the wall of the church, saying: "House to let for 5 ducats" (*Casa da fitar Ducati 5*).

Bibliography: S.M.M., 1955, p. 134.

162. *Miraculous cure of the daughter of Benvegnudo da San Polo*
Canvas, 359 × 296 cm (cat. n. 562)
Acquisition: 1820, following the suppression edicts
Last restored: 1958-1960

Another of the School of St. John the Evangelist series (see previous entry), this painting illustrates the miraculous cure in 1414 of Benvegnudo's daughter. Paralysed from birth, she was cured on touching three small candles which her father had placed near to the relic of the Cross. The episode, set in a Renaissance-style hall, reveals a scene of great historic interest recalling the compositions of Carpaccio in the St. Ursula series. This provides the earliest possible date for the work. In a letter which is being delivered by a young man in the foreground the words "Spettabili domino Franc... fidelis" are distinguishable. But Zanotto stated (1833-1834) that he had also read the name "Duodo" on it, which would place the date around 1506, a Francesco Duodo then being "Head Guardian" of the School. In any case, the work must be among those that were executed after 1502 when the Senate granted permission to the School to take on another 50 members with the object of increasing funds available for the decoration of the Sala dell'Albergo.

Bibliography: S.M.M., 1955, p. 137, n. 144; V. Moschini, 1960, p. 358; S. Mason Rinaldi, 1978, pp. 299-300; J.G. Bernasconi, 1981, p. 201.

Mantegna, Andrea
Island of Cartura 1431 - Mantua 1506

163. *St. George*
Panel, 66 × 32 cm (cat. n. 588)
Acquisition: 1856, by purchase from the Manfrin collection
Last restored: 1933

In a good state of preservation but with slight retouching of the armour and the dragon's face. The provenance of the work is unknown, though it is thought that it was originally the side panel of a group.
Art critics have suggested various dates approximating to the frescoes of the Eremitani (Augustinian Friars), to the altarpiece of San Zeno or to Mantegna's first years in Mantua. Today they almost unanimously favour a date coinciding with the artist's stay in Florence between 1466 and 1467. Indeed the imperturbable young saint and mythological hero rather than exponent of Christian piety reflects the artist's Florentine education in the tactile, almost chiselled clarity of Donatello's example. Reference to past history is evoked while a keen awareness of the future is instilled into this humanistic study of serenity and handsome beauty which seems to derive from the experiments of the Tuscan contemporaries of Mantegna.

Bibliography: S.M.M., 1955, pp. 139-140, n. 148; N. Garavaglia, 1967, p. 99.

Marco Antonio di Ruggero (?)
(Zoppo, Marco) (?)
Cento 1453 - Venice 1478

164. *The Saviour giving his Blessing between SS. Vincenzo Ferreri, Augustine, Helen and Francis*
Canvas, 136 × 407 cm
(cat. ns. 614, 622, 620)
Inscription: .MCCCCLVIII - ADI - II°GENER, the date 1468 on step of throne
Acquisition: 1838, from depository of the Commenda at Malta following the suppression edicts
Last restored: now in course

Originally in the Cavatter Magistracy at the Doge's Palace, this large canvas was split up and not until 1948 was it reassembled after adding two strips along the lines of the floor and the pilasters. The four major coats of arms are evidently those of magistrates in office at the time, while the smaller ones along the base are later additions. Sharing the same provenance and mark of the Paduan-Mantegnesque school with n. 272 below, and even though the qualitative level is higher here, this canvas has been attributed to the workshop of Giovanni Bellini. But in the light of present restoration the formal tensity of expression and the linear representation of the figures would seem to match better with the work of Marco Zoppo. They are remarkably similar to the figures in his Pesaro altarpiece (Staatliche Museum, Berlin) which Zoppo painted in Venice in 1471.

Bibliography: S.M.M., 1955, pp. 89-90, n. 85.

Marconi, Rocco
records from 1504 - d. 1529

165. *Christ and the adulteress*
Oil on canvas, 131 × 197 cm
(cat. n. 1306)
Inscription: ROCHUS / MARCHONIUS, a
notice on the central column
Acquisition: 1947, from the Royal
Palace, Venice

Recorded as being in the Chapter Hall
of the Monastery of San Giorgio Maggiore, this picture, which became State
property during the Napoleonic sequestration, is one of the many versions
of a theme dear to Rocco Marconi and
his workshop. It is clear that it was
painted in a late period of the aritst's activities for it shows the influence of Palma
il Vecchio and of Pordenone.

Bibliography: S.M.M., 1962, p. 137, n.
220.

Marescalco, Giovanni
see Buonconsiglio, Giovanni

Marieschi, Michele
Venice 1710-1744

166. *Courtyard with Stairs*
Oil on canvas, 41 × 57 cm
(cat. n. 451)
Acquisition: 1816, by legacy of
Girolamo Molin
Last restored: 1958

A work of Marieschi's youthful years
when he was much taken up in perspective studies of value to his activities as
a stage designer.

Bibliography: S.M.M., 1970, p. 55, n.
117; E. Young, 1977, p. 3 *et seq.*

167. *Imaginary Scene with Bridge*
Oil on canvas, 61 × 95 cm
(cat. n. 715)
Acquisition: 1908, by purchase from
the antiquarian C. Balboni
Last restored: 1958

Marieschi's views show the mark of his
work as a designer of stage scenery. They
are sometimes "real", but more often
born of fantasy, as here where beyond
the bridge we see a turreted city with the
ruins of an old building in the background.

Bibliography: S.M.M., 1970, pp. 55-56,
n. 118.

168. *Imaginary Scene with Arch*
Oil on canvas, 55 × 83 cm
(cat. n. 727)
Acquisition: 1903, by purchase from
Countess Elena Prine di Breganze
Last restored: 1962

This and the imaginary view that accompanies it reveals the unspoilt freshness of
Marieschi's painting which at once brings
to mind the fleeting touch of Mario Ricci's work and the delicacy of Zuccarelli's
palette.

Bibliography: S.M.M., 1970, p. 56, n.
119.

169. *Imaginary Scene with Obelisk*
Oil on canvas, 55 × 83 cm
(cat. n. 728)
Acquisition: 1903, by purchase from
Countess Elena Prine di Breganze
Last restored: 1962

Even more so than in the preceding work
a "quadrangular" view opens up before
us: one in which imagined and real
details are synthesised and given unity
in a scenic presentation achieved by
delicate colour shading. The colours
change slowly from the brilliance of the
foreground to an increasingly diaphanous
transparency as the eye wanders over the
luminous country scene in the background.

Bibliography: S.M.M., 1970, p. 56, n.
120.

Marinetti, Antonio
(Il Chiozzotto)
Chioggia 1719 - Venice 1796

170. *St. Luke*
Oil on canvas, 147 × 79 cm
(cat. n. 1362)
Acquisition: 1807, from the Old
Academy of Venice
Last restored: 1969

The set piece for his entry as a member
of the Academy, this picture once hung
in the Assembly Hall of the Venice
Academy together with Pittoni's *Annunciation* (see entry n. 216) and *St. Mark*
by Angeli (see n. 5). The inking of the
dark shading and the blending of the
tones call attention to Chiozzotto's attachment to examples of Maestro Piazzetta's
work in the 1740s.

Bibliography: U. Ruggeri, 1983, p. 170,
n. 73.

Marziale, Marco
records from 1493 to 1507

171. *The Supper at Emmaus*
Panel, 122 × 141 cm (cat. n. 76)
Inscription: MARCUS MARCIALIS /
VENETUS / 1506, on a sign on table leg
Acquisition: 1838, by gift of Girolamo
Contarini
Last restored: 1979

The pictorial antecedent of this work,
which in its details shows Düreresque inspiration, must be Giovanni Bellini's
destroyed *Cena in Emaus* recorded by
Vasari as being in the Giorgio Cornaro
collection (1568) and known through an
engraving made of it by Pietro Monaco.
A copy of this engraving survives in the
Venetian Church of San Salvador.
Another variant of the same subject was
painted by Marziale in 1507 and is now
in the Berlin Museum.

Bibliography: S.M.M., 1955, p. 143, n.
153.

Mazzoni, Sebastiano
Florence c. 1611 - Venice 1678

172. *Annunciation*
Oil on canvas, 154 × 112 cm
(cat. n.1329)
Acquisition: 1945, from the State-
owned church of Santa Caterina
Last restored: 1956

A work of the 1640s, this *Annunciation*
was noted in the Venetian Church of
Santa Caterina at the beginning of the
19th century. It is possibly the same one
that Boschini refers to in 1664 as being
in the church of San Luca in Venice. To
the fanciful and exuberant painting of
Maffei in his decorative vein Sebastiano
Mazzoni reacts with a talent just as free
and fanciful but with an intellectual content that seems to reflect the early Tuscan
education of this artist.

Bibliography: S.M.M., 1970, p. 58, n.
126.

Meldolla, Andrea
(Schiavone)
Žara 1522 - Venice 1563

173. *The Presentation of Jesus in the Temple*
Oil on canvas, 118 × 215 cm
(cat. n. 324)

Acquisition: 1838, by gift of Girolamo Contarini

Last restored: 1958

Certainly one of his late works, this picture is marked by measured, slow-moving rhythms of a narrative told in the manneristic style of the Tiziano of about ten years previous to 1560, which is judged to be the approximate date of the painting.

Bibliography: S.M.M., 1962, p. 191, n. 320; F.L. Richardson, 1980, p. 173.

174. *Deucalion and Pyrrha*
Oil on panel, 41 × 118 cm
(cat. n. 713)

Acquisition: 1904, by purchase from the antiquarian D. Barozzi of Venice

Deucalion and Pyrrha are throwing stones over their shoulders to create men and women after a mythological deluge had engulfed the earth. This and the panel that follows may be the two paintings referred to by Edwards as being in the collection of the brothers Dolfin at Malcanton. Here the manneristic elegance of Parmigianino has fallen lightly on the shoulders of Schiavone with decorative and pleasing results. Recently, together with the panel below (entry n. 175), this picture has, however, been tentatively ascribed to Bonifacio Veronese (see de' Pitati).

Bibliography: S.M.M., 1962, p. 190, n. 318; F.L. Richardson, 1980, p. 201.

175. *The Judgement of Midas*
Oil on panel, 40 × 118 cm
(cat. n. 714)

Acquisition: 1904, by purchase from the antiquarian D. Barozzi of Venice

No less than in the previous picture this one is representative of Schiavone's decorative style and his open-ended brush which is rich in light and leans heavily on the flowing sinuousness of Bonifacio Veronese's colour tones.

Bibliography: S.M.M., 1962, p. 190, n. 317; F.L. Richardson, 1980, p. 201.

Meldolla, Andrea
(attributed to)

176. *Allegory of Nature*
Oil on panel, 42 × 74 cm
(cat. n. 901)
Acquisition: from the Royal Palace, Venice
Last restored: 1960

Recorded as being in the Mint in 1788, it was moved to the Royal Palace in the early 1900s. The attribution of this painting to Schiavone has recently been put in doubt in favour of the workshop of Bonifacio Veronese.

Bibliography: S.M.M., 1962, p. 190, n. 319; F.L. Richardson, 1980, p. 201.

Memling, Hans
Selingestadt am Main 1435/1440 -
Bruges 1494

177. *Portrait of a Young Man*
Panel, 26 × 20 cm (cat. n. 586)
Acquisition: 1856, by purchase from the Manfrin collection
Last restored: 1949

For long attributed to Antonello da Messina, in 1871 Cavalcaselle pointed out how like this work was to *Portrait of a Man in a fur coat*, Uffizi Gallery, and to Memling's *Portrait of a Man with medal* in Antwerp. Later critics, also the Catalogue of 1903, quite definitely endorsed a verdict favouring Memling. It is one of a group of similar portraits dating from 1470 to 1480, the closest of which would appear to be *The Young Man* in the Corsini Gallery, Florence. The meek and thoughtful face and the hand

lightly resting on an invisible parapet — the latter motif was to become dear to Giorgione and his circle — are set against a partially illuminated background which in no way disturbs the feeling of tranquillity that the artist conveys.
A humanistic work which reaches beyond national boundaries to unite Memling to the classical ideal of beauty and dignity common to all the figurative arts in the last decades of the Quattrocento.

Bibliography: S.M.M., 1955, p. 183, n. 206; G.T. Faggin, 1969, p. 110.

Michele di Matteo
active between 1410 and c. 1470

178. *Polyptych*
In central row: *Madonna enthroned adoring the Child, with four angels*; to left, *SS. Lucia and Helen*; to right, *Mary Magdalene and Catherine of Alexandria*. In the coping: four panels with *Doctors of the Church* and, central panel, *The Crucifixion*; left, *the Evangelists SS. Matthew and Mark*; right, *SS. John and Luke*. In band separating the two rows: seventeen small mouldings with the *Redeemer* and *Saints*. In the predella five accounts of the finding of the true Cross: from left, *St. Helen arrives in Jerusalem and convenes the Jews who take counsel together - Judah does not wish to show her where the Cross is - when lowered into a well he reveals and unearths it himself - as*

proof that it is the true Cross a dead child is raised - adoration of the Cross while devils flee
Panels: the polyptych is composed of two orders separated by a central fascia, 21 × 225 cm, and by a superimposed predella 32 × 1.25 cm. Each order is made up of three panels: in the upper row a central panel, 111 × 64 cm, in the lower row a central panel, 142 × 63 cm; the lateral panels in the upper row are 111 × 85 cm and in the lower 142 × 82 cm (cat. n. 24)
Inscription: MICHAEL MATHEI DA BONONIA F. . at the foot of St. Catherine
Acquisition: 1812, following the suppression decrees
Last restored: 1979

This polyptych comes from the Church of Sant'Elena where its place was on the altar dedicated to that saint erected in 1418 by Alessandro Borromei.
Although restored in 1829, the structure is mainly original work. Masterpiece of the Bolognese artist di Matteo, it was executed after 1427 in which year a wooden crucifix is known to have been standing at the centre of the altar. It was probably Prior Fra Bernardo de' Scapi, himself a Bolognese, who gave di Matteo the commission. The sinuous rhythm, precious elegance and rich decoration make this one of the most charming creations of Italian painting of the late Middle Ages. The pleasing freshness of the small picture stories in the predella is of special note.

Bibliography: S.M.M., 1955, pp. 172-173, n. 195.

Michieli, Andrea
(Vicentino)
Vicenza c. 1542 - c. 1617

179. *Paradise*
Oil on canvas, 116 × 86 cm
(cat. n. 1354)
Acquisition: 1978, by purchase from Maria Laro and Piero Scarpa

Dating from the beginning of the Seicento, this is the first preliminary study for the *Paradiso* in the Church of Santa Maria Gloriosa dei Frari of which another version is now to be seen in the Walker Gallery at Liverpool. The influence of Tintoretto is apparent in this crowded composition which embraces a very wide variety of lighting and colour effects. Tintoretto was the Cinquecento artist who was most admired by painters of "the seven styles" and Vicentino their outstanding representative.

Bibliography: T. Mullay, 1964, p. 507 *et seq.*

Migliara, Giovanni
Alessandria 1785 - Milan 1837

180. *View of a church on the lagoon shore*
Oil on canvas, 45 × 56 cm
(cat. n. 710)
Acquisition: 1903, by purchase from Romeo Gottardo of Venice
Last restored: 1962

At various times thought to be by Guardi or Canaletto, this picture is now rightly attributed to Migliara in the years 1814 to 1817 when the trend was moving against the great Venetian masters of panoramic views of the 18th century.

Bibliography: S.M.M., 1970, p. 212, n. 52.

Mola, Pierfrancesco
Coldré 1617-1666

181. *Allegory of the phlegmatic temperament*
Oil on canvas, 76 × 114 cm
(cat. n. 1314)
Acquisition: 1955, by purchase from Signora Violet Ravà Fenton

An allegory which reverts to the *Iconologia* in which Ripa postulates the existence of four elements in the human temperament (Padua, 1630). Here the man sleeping beside the water symbolises the phlegmatic temperament.
In the figure of the slumbering Turk Mola blends his youthful formation, after Guercino, with neo-Venetian tendencies which he developed during his first stay in the Serenissima before 1637.

Bibliography: S.M.M., 1970, p. 144, n. 319.

Montagna, Bartolomeo
see Cincani, Bartolomeo

Moranzone, Jacopo

records from 1430 - d. between 10
April 1467 and 24 November 1469

182. *Polyptych*
In central panel: *Our Lady of the
Assumption*; in the side panels: *SS.
Helen, John the Baptist, Benedict and
Elisabeth*
Five panels, gold background:
central, 138 × 59 cm; lateral, each
125 × 33 cm (cat. n. 11)
Acquisition: 1812, following the
suppression edicts
Last restored: 1952

Once in the Church of Sant'Elena for
which it was painted with part of a legacy
left in 1441 by Donna Elisabetta, mother
of Fra Tommaso of Venice. Several
sources refer to an inscription with
signature and the date 1441, perhaps
originally on the wooden cornice. Mentioned by Vasari as the only painting wor-
thy of mention by this artist, who, he
says, "paints all his figures on their tip-
toes".
The Gothic-style positioning of the
figures, influenced by Michele di Matteo's

polyptych for the same church (see entry
n. 178) shows scant recognition of new
developments that were maturing at the
time in Venice. And there is a certain
roughness in the contours, as in intaglio
work, which in fact the Moranzone family
had long practised.

Bibliography: S.M.M., 1955, pp. 31-32,
n. 29.

Moretti, Giuseppe

a native of Val Camonica, active in
Venice in the second half of the 18th
century

183. *Perspective*
Oil on canvas, 130 × 56 cm
(cat. n. 471)
Acquisition: 1807, from the Old
Academy of Venice

Exhibited at the Sensa Festival in 1777,
this painting was given to the Academy
by the perspective artist Moretti on his
admission to membership in that year.
The architectural features recall Canaletto, though they are of a more classical
derivation. And the figures even more so:
they take after those of Canaletto's great
masterpiece *Campo di San Giacomo di
Rialto*, now in the Staatliche Museum in
Berlin.

Bibliography: S.M.M., 1970, p. 60, n.
130.

Moretto, Alessandro
see Bonvicino, Alessandro

Morlaiter, Michelangelo
Venice 1729-1806

184. *Venice rewards the Fine Arts*
Oil on canvas, 131 × 183 cm
(cat. n. 425)
Acquisition: 1807, from the Old
Academy of Venice
Last restored: 1960

Exhibited at the Sensa Festival of 1777, this picture was very probably given to the Academy by Morlaiter at the time of his admission. It shows Venice awarding prizes to pupils of Painting, Sculpture and Architecture. An academic subject painted in the manneristic style by now well tempered by neo-classical frigidity.

Bibliography: S.M.M., 1970, p. 60, n. 130.

Morone, Francesco
Verona 1471-1529

185. *Madonna and Child with St. Rocco*
Detached fresco transferred to canvas, 118 × 113 cm (cat. n. 735)
Inscription: MDXVII - ADI VII AVOSTO/ [GESÙ E LA S]UA MADRE VERZENE MARIA, BERNARDI[n] QSER - [CORADIN FATO] FAR - QUESTA OPA P - SUO VODO E DEVOTION -, at base, the words shown in brackets having been copied by Da Persico in 1820
Acquisition: 1908, by purchase from the antiquarian Carlo Balboni
Last restored: when transferred in 1908

Incomplete on the left side and with some painted areas missing, this fresco was removed from a house at Cassano di Tramigna in the Verona Province. It is attributed to Morone, in particular for the similarity it shows to the full and restful colouring of the *Madonna col Bambino* in the "Santa Casa" fresco painted two years before in 1517 and now in the Castelvecchio Museum at Verona.

Bibliography: S.M.M., 1955, p. 147.

Muttoni, Pietro
(Vecchia, della, Pietro)
Venice 1603-1678

186. *Votive picture*
Oil on canvas, 285 × 227 cm
(cat. n. 868)
Inscription: EX VOTO, in centre at base; PVF 1640, on right
Acquisition: following the suppression edicts
Last restored: 1961

Originally in the Venetian Church of Santa Giustina, this very large canvas which is dated 1640, alludes perhaps to a conversion. St. Giustina looks on from the distant sky while in the foreground an angel shows a skull symbolic of the transience of earthly things to the bejewelled lady sitting at the top of the steps. To either side of her are St. Joseph and St. John the Baptist. In a solemn and dignified scene very much of Cinquecento taste the statuesque figure of the angel approaches the astonished lady in a dramatic baroque manner. The extreme liveliness and creative fantasy of the artist are indicative of the brilliant imaginative powers of Muttoni. He was known as "della Vecchia" for his skill as a restorer and imitator of works by great Venetian painters of the Cinquecento, expecially those of Giorgione and Tiziano.

Bibliography: S.M.M., 1970, p. 118, n. 255; B. Aikema, 1982, pp. 89-90.

Negretti, Jacopo
(Palma, Jacopo il Giovane)
Venice c. 1550 -1628

187. *The Crucifixion of St. Peter*
Oil on canvas, 168 × 132 cm
(cat. n. 660)
Acquisition: 1901, by gift of M.
Guggenheim

Dating from about 1615, this is clearly the preliminary painting for a ceiling. It is an excellent example of Palma il Giovane's "conservative" tendencies which led him to re-evoke a selective choice of the great ideas of Venetian painters of the second half of the Cinquecento: Tiziano, Paolo Veronese and in particular Jacopo Tintoretto.

Bibliography: S.M.M., 1962, p. 151, n. 249; S. Mason Rinaldi, 1984, p. 137, n. 516.

Negretti, Jacopo
(Palma, Jacopo il Vecchio)
Serina, Bergamo c. 1480 - Venice 1528

188. *The Assumption*
Oil on panel, 191 × 137 cm
(cat. n. 315)
Acquisition: 1812, following the suppression edicts
Last restored: 1963

Originally in the School of Santa Maria Maggiore, Venice, this is a panel of Palma il Vecchio's early years when he declared himself to be under the influence of the new painting of Giorgione and the splendid version of this subject offered by Tiziano.

Bibliography: S.M.M., 1962, p. 160 *et seq.*, n. 271; G. Mariacher, 1975, p. 215; Ph. Rylands, 1977, pp. 245-250; AA.VV., *Riflettoscopia...*, 1984, pp. 54-59.

189. *Sacred Conversation*
Oil on canvas, 127 × 195 cm
(cat. n. 147)
Acquisition: 1900, by purchase from Alessandro Bedendo of Mestre
Last restored: 1956

Listed in the Pizzamano collection, this painting is almost certainly one referred to by Ridolfi in 1648 and by Martinioni in 1663 as being in the house of Widman of Venice. The rich colour texture and restful rhythm of the composition reveals the influence of Tiziano's classical sense of chromatics on this masterpiece by Palma il Vecchio. The artist died while painting it, as is shown by the unfinished hands of John the Baptist and St. Catherine. It was perhaps completed by Vecellio himself, as the head of the saint and the landscape with castle suggest, X-ray photography having shown the superior quality and different technique of these details in comparison with Palma's own. A recent examination by reflectoscope has brought to light the arch of a colonnade in a first draft beneath the painting.

Bibliography: S.M.M., 1962, p. 162 *et seq.*, n. 273; G. Mariacher, 1975, p. 215.

Nicola di Maestro Antonio d'Ancona
active between 1460 and c. 1485

190. *The Crucifixion*
Panel, 101 × 70 cm (cat. n. 51)
Acquisition: 1816, by legacy from Girolamo Molin
Last restored: now in course

This painting, which during the last century remained for a long time in depositories, has been the subject of many attributions all of which ascribe it to Paduan artists, notably to those who had learned their art in Squarcione's workshop. So it was thought until in 1947 Roberto Longhi reported it to be an early work by this artist from the Marches of Italy whose formation developed parallel with that of Schiavone, Tura and Crivelli. In all probability it is to be placed at the end of the 1460s as warping caused by Mantegna's predella of San Zeno can be seen. "One of the most cruel and obsessive of paintings", it has been said, in which the miniature rendering of a distant Jerusalem seems to be inspired by Flemish art, for example, by Van Eyck's *Crucifixion* in the Ca' d'Oro.

Bibliography: S.M.M., 1955, p. 150, n. 165; F. Zeri, 1958, p. 38.

Nicolò di Pietro
active between 1389 and 1416 - still living in 1430

191. *Madonna and Child enthroned, with angels playing music and the donor, Fulciano Belgarzone di Zara; as figures on the shoulders of the throne, the announcing Angel and the Virgin Mary*
Panel, gold background, 107 × 65 cm (cat. n. 19)
Inscription: HOC / OPUS / FECIT F̄IĒI / D̄N̄S VULC̄IA / BELGARÇONE / CIVIS.YA/DRIENSIS. / MCCCLXXXXIIII. NICHOLA. / FILIUS M̄R̄I PETRI PICTORIS DE VENE/CHS. PINXIT HOC OPUS QUI MO/RATUR IN CHAPITE PONTIS PARADINI; under the throne dais are the signature, the date and name of the donor
Acquisition: 1856, by purchase from the Manfrin collection
Last restored: 1949

The first known dated work by this artist. It is a picture of some significance in the transition phase between the Trecento and the Quattrocento. It shows that so far from being passively conformist Nicolò was well acquainted with current Bohemian and Emilian art styles. Here there is in fact much to show a leaning on his part towards a new concept of perspective and colour. At the same time the serene bonhomie of the Madonna is a thoroughly Bolognese characteristic.

Bibliography: S.M.M., 1955, p. 14, n. 10; A. Scarpa Sonino, 1975-1976, pp. 781-782.

192. *St. Laurence*
Panel, gold background, with plaster adornments, 62 × 22 cm (cat. n. 20)
Acquisition: 1816, by legacy from Ascanio Molin
Last restored: 1951

Probably the surviving panel of an altarpiece, this painting perhaps dates from the second decade of the Quattrocento and therefore belongs to the last phase of Nicolò's active life as an artist. A return to nordic elements is to be noted, and these are seen to be in common with his *St. Ursula* in the New York Metropolitan Museum of Art.

Bibliography: S.M.M., 1955, p. 14-15, n. 11; A. Scarpa Sonino, 1975-1976, p. 782.

Nogari, Giuseppe
Venice c. 1700-1763

193. *Old Woman with bowl*
Oil on canvas, 52 × 41 cm
(cat. n. 1315)
Acquisition: 1953, by gift of
Francesco Pospisil

A typical example of the character studies
which Nogari often painted, but one in
which natural detail loses its true-life ring
to take on the colour of decorative stereotyped features.

Bibliography: S.M.M., 1970, p. 63, n.
134.

Novelli, Pier Antonio
Venice 1729-1804

194. *Design, Colour and Creativity*
Oil on canvas, 130 × 182 cm
(cat. n. 762)

Inscription: PETRUS ANTONIUS NOVELLI /
VENETUS PINXIT ANNO 1776, at lower
right

Acquisition: 1807, from the Old
Academy of Venice

Last restored: 1960

A painting revised in 1776 which the artist first executed in about 1771 after being elected to the Academy at its sitting
of 8 May 1768. Both the composition
and colour work of this allegory are well-
founded on prevailing neo-classical ideas.

Bibliography: S.M.M., 1970, p. 63,
R.135.

Palma, Jacopo il Giovane
see Negretti, Jacopo

Palma, Jacopo il Vecchio
see Negretti, Jacopo

Pantaleon (?)
active c. 1460

195. *The Nativity*
Panel, 77 × 52 cm (cat. n. 720)
Acquisition: 1906, by gift of Casimiro Sipriot of Marseilles
Last restored: 1979

This and the painting immediately following have generally been attributed to a Venetian artist in the circle of Gentile da Fabriano and Jacopo Bellini, but to one who in the past has been variously named. The discovery in a private collection in Paris of a similar version of *The Nativity* signed *"M. . . . Pantaleon pinsit 1460"* has led to the attribution of both pictures to this master. Two other replicas with varying inscriptions are in the hands of collectors in Paris and New York. Compared with these, the two paintings treated here seem to be of a late and more developed phase of the artist's work characterised by an ingenuous narrative spirit close to the figurative style of Jacopo Bellini and Antonio Vivarini, who at the time were still under the spell of the international Gothic style.

Bibliography: S.M.M., 1955, p. 33, n. 32; R. Pallucchini, 1959-1960, pp. 196-198.

196. *Madonna and Child with winged Angels and the Annunciation* in the pendentives
Panel, gold background, 49 × 35 cm (cat. n. 48)
Inscription: GENTILE FABRIANENSIS F., apocryphal signature on parapet at base
Acquisition: 1816, by legacy of Ascanio Molin
Last restored: 1979

A modest work not, however, without a certain pleasant charm. See previous entry.

Bibliography: S.M.M., 1955, p. 33, n. 31; R. Pallucchini, 1959-1960, p. 198; C.L. Ragghianti, 1977, p. 232.

Paolo Veneziano
active 1333 to 1358 - d. previous to September 1362

197. *Madonna and Child enthroned, with two donors*
Panel, gold background, 142 × 90 cm in the original frame 157 × 105 cm (cat. n. 786)
Acquisition: 1913, by purchase from the antiquarian Salvadori of Venice
Last restored: 1952

While still retaining its original dentil frame and the old cross pieces on the back, this work has lost the flesh tints and some of the colouring of the Virgin's clothes, also the inscription beneath. Recognised as one of Paolo's pictures since the cataloguing of 1928, it is now universally accepted as such. With its closeness to the altar frontal at Dignano (1321), which may have been painted slightly earlier, it can confidently be placed in the second half of the third decade of the Trecento. The Madonna with the tiny Christ Child in the clipeus is the Syrian iconographic device of the Platytera, while the suggestion of welcoming to her mantle the two pious figures, lower left, whose characterised features indicate that they are miniature portraits, is an unusual reminder of the *Madonna della Misericordia*. The inspiring figure, the harmonious blending of oriental and western effects and the richness of the colours combine to confirm the view that this is Paolo Veneziano's masterpiece.

Bibliography: S.M.M., 1955, pp. 16-17, n. 13; M. Muraro, 1969, pp. 43, 147; R. Pallucchini, 1974, n. 87.

198. Polyptych
In central panel: *The Coronation of
the Virgin*; in the side panels, left: *the
Adoration of the Magi, the Baptism of
Christ, the Last Supper, the Agony in
the Garden and the Capture of Christ*;
in side panels, right: *the Procession to
Calvary and meeting with the Holy
Mother, the Crucifixion, Resurrection,
"Noli me tangere" ("Touch me not")
and Ascension*. In the coping, from
left: *Pentecost, St. Matthew, the
clothing of St. Clare, St. John, St.
Francis renders his clothes to his
father, St. Francis receives the
stigmata, St. Mark, Death of St.
Francis, St. Luke, Christ the Judge*; at
centre: the two prophets *Isaiah and
David*
Panels, gold background: central,
98 × 63 cm; four lateral, each
40 × 94 cm; in coping, 26 × 19 cm,
the six larger panels of 26 × 19 cm,
the four minor ones of 23 × 7 cm;
the two top ones 30 × 16 cm
(cat. n. 21)

Acquisition: 1812, following the
suppression edicts. The central panel,
mistakenly taken to the Brera
Gallery, Milan, in 1808, was restored
to its original place only in 1950
Last restored: 1951

Painted and constructed for the Venetian
Church of Santa Chiara, as confirmed by
the figures of Franciscan monks in the
coping and, in particular, by the panel
of *The Death of St. Francis* with the small
figure of a nun, who may be the donor.
The framework, perhaps partly rear-
ranged, is the original one and the polyptych as a whole is complete, though
possibly a *Crucifixion* may be missing
from the summit. The attribution of the
work to Paolo was affirmed by the
Catalogue of 1924 and later definitely
recognised after Frick's comparisons with
The Coronation of the Virgin of 1358.
Some reservations have been expressed
in regard to the lateral panels in which
the hand of workshop assistants has been
discerned. But the quality of these panels

does not really justify such a supposition
since the artist, if anything, in develop-
ing the scriptural episodes may have
changed his elegantly aulic Byzantine
style, adopted in the central panel, to
more precise allusions to western concepts. In any case, this is a composite,
if apparently contradictory figurative interpretation, and it is transmitted to us
in brilliantly glowing colour.

Bibliography: S.M.M., 1955, pp. 15-16,
n. 12; R. Pallucchini, 1964, pp. 45-48;
M. Muraro, 1969, pp. 147-148; S. Borla,
1970, nn. 201-202.

Parisati, Jacopo
recorded from 1458 - d. between 20
April and 14 August 1499

**199a,b. *The Archangel Gabriel, Our
Lady of the Annunciation***
Two partial panels, 185 × 74 cm and
185 × 76 cm (cat. ns. 606, 608)
Acquisition: 1812, following the
suppression edicts
Last restored: 1984

Once in the Church of Santa Maria at
Monteortone, near Padua, these two
panels are rightly attributed to the
traducer of Mantegna's legacy of a
decorative linear style in favour of artistic
changes initiated by Giovanni Bellini.
They are not therefore without a refined
delicacy adapted to surrounding perspective which suggest a knowledge of the
inlay work of Pietro Antonio degli Abati.
Most probably painted when Parisati was
engaged on frescoes at Monteortone, that
is between 1494 and 1497, the panels
have very recently been restored. This
has freed them of a greyish coat of paint
applied at some time to the background
areas. Its removal has revealed colour
elements previously unsuspected and of
a lively warmth that may be of nordic
inspiration.

Bibliography: S.M.M., 1955, p 132, n.
136; C. Nepi Sciré, 1985.

Parisati, Jacopo (?)

200. *Our Lady of Sorrows*
Panel. 47 × 30 cm (cat. n. 587)
Acquisition: 1816, by legacy of
Girolamo Molin
Last restored: 1979

Usually regarded as portraying *Our Lady
of Sorrows*, this painting might equally
well be of a holy nun. When acquired
by these Galleries it was thought to be
by Antonello da Messina but was soon
assigned to the Paduan school as it was
possible, though by no means certain, to
see in this panel the influence of the later
work of Jacopo da Montagnana.

Bibliography: S.M.M., 1955, p. 133, n.
137.

Pellegrini, Domenico
Galliera, Bassano 1759 - Rome 1840

201. *Portrait of the engraver
Francesco Bartolozzi*
Oil on canvas, 166 × 88 cm
(cat. n. 453)
Acquisition: 1834, by gift of the
author
Last restored: 1958

Painted in London in about 1744, this
is a portrait of Francesco Bartolozzi who
was a member of the Venice Academy
and patron of Pellegrini in London, he,
too, being elected to the Academy in
1796. In the Gallery catalogues of 1895
and 1903, in which it was attributed
respectively to Reynolds and Romney,
this portrait is indeed typical of the
mature work of Pellegrini. The artist was
particularly attentive, especially in portraiture, to that free and lively interpretation practised by his English contemporaries.

Bibliography: S.M.M., 1970, p. 74, n.
159.

Pellegrini, Giovanni Antonio
Venice 1675-1741

202. *Painting*
Oil on canvas, 142 × 132 cm
(cat. n. 1319)
Acquisition: 1959, by purchase from
Count Alvise Giustiniani of Venice
Last restored: 1959

In painting this symbolic figure Pellegrini
used a brush rich in shades of silver applied with delicate toning. It puts one in
mind of the pastel work of his sister-in-
law Rosalba Carriera.

Bibliography: S.M.M., 1970, p. 75, n.
161.

203. *Sculpture*
Oil on canvas, 142 × 132 cm
(cat. n.1320)
Acquisition: 1959, by purchase from
Count Alvise Giustiniani of Venice
Last restored: 1959

The allegory of *Sculpture* and its companion piece *Painting* (see entry n. 202) were painted towards the end of the 1720s. They represent the refined and elegant work of Giovanni Antonio Pellegrini who was one of the pioneers of international rococo painting and of its light and superficial aspirations.

Bibliography: S.M.M., 1970, p. 75, n. 160.

Pennacchi, Pier Maria
1464 - 1514/1515

204. *The Death of the Virgin Mary*
Panel, 134 × 169 cm (cat. n. 657)
Inscription: (PE)TRUS (M)ARIA,
fragmentary signature on step at base
Acquisition: 1907, by purchase from
the Seminary at Udine which
acquired it from the Cernazai
collection. Since 1903 it had been
held on deposit
Last restored: 1948

By general agreement this work is of the artist's late maturity since it comes close in style to the frescoes which he painted on commission (1511) with Salvador Mundi on the semi-dome of the Santissimo chapel in Treviso Cathedral. Noteworthy for its compositional fullness, it shows clear derivative connections with Lotto and Pseudo-Boccaccio's *Washing of the feet* (see entry n. 125). The chromatic effects cannot now be fully appreciated owing to some erosion of the paint layers, but there remains much of the tonal quality.

Bibliography: S.M.M., 1955, pp. 147-148, n. 160; D. Gioseffi, 1978, p. 98; C. Nepi Sciré, *Il pittore trevigiano...*, 1980, pp. 38-39.

Piazzetta, Giambattista
Venice 1683-1754

205. *Christ crucified between the two thieves*
Oil on canvas, 76 × 62 cm
(cat. n. 162)
Acquisition: 1905, by purchase from
the antiquarian Sebastiano Candrian

Dating from 1710 this picture is one of the first entries in Piazzetta's catalogue. In the heavy, dark shading and in the sharp tension of the lighting the artist expresses himself with dramatic force. In doing so he draws away from the ''naturalistic'' idiom of his master, Giuseppe Maria Crespi.

Bibliography: S.M.M., 1970, p. 75, n. 162; A. Mariuz (with Foreword by R. Pallucchini), 1982, p. 75 *et seq.*, n. 4.

206. *Crucifix*
Oil on canvas, 72 × 51 cm
(cat. n . 809)
Acquisition: 1923, by purchase from
the Convent of Santa Maria della
Fava

Originally in the St. Philip Neri Oratory
attached to the Venetian Church of Santa
Maria della Fava, this painting must be
dated at about 1720 for the perfection
of its colour qualities and the finer
modulation of its plasticity in comparison
with the work of the artist in his younger
years.

Bibliography: S.M.M., 1970, p. 75, n.
163; A. Mariuz (with Foreword by R.
Pallucchini), 1982, p. 79, n. 19.

207. *The Enigma*
Oil on canvas, 154 × 114 cm
(cat. n. 483)
Inscription: ISCRITTIONE SEPOLCRALE DEL
FAMOSO PITTOR PIAZZETTA AUTORE DI
QUESTO QUADRO FATTOLI FARE A VENEZIA
IL 1740; E PAGATO ZECCHINI QUINDICI, on
an 18th century folio attached in the
back of the canvas, and with it a
funeral inscription
Acquisition: by purchase from dealer
Ehrenfreund
Last restored: 1983

The picture was painted at a time of the
artist's life when he definitely broke with
his youthful fidelity to a severe chiaroscuro style and adopted a sensual range
of colour tones stressed by strong lighting
effects, by their "sunniness", as his contemporaries noted. From whites, browns,
greenish and pale pink hues the lighter
colours project the figure of a peasant girl
who is holding a puppy beneath her left
arm. All is set out in a well studied composition of rhythms and figurative devices
so that the real-life content takes on the
nature of a pastoral idyll which has been
interpreted in a number of ways. A recent suggestion is that this sensual young
wanton was intended to symbolise Venetian civilization in the twilight of its splendour.

Bibliography: S.M.M., 1970, p. 76, n.
164; M. Mariuz (with Foreword by R.
Pallucchini), 1982, p. 95 *et seq.*, n. 95;
U. Ruggeri, 1983, p. 102 *et seq.*, n. 35.

Piero della Francesca
Borgo San Sepolcro 1415/1420-1492

208. *St. Jerome and a devotee*
Panel, 49 × 42 cm (cat. n. 47)
Inscription: PETRI DE BŪ/GO SCI
SEP/ULCRI OPUS., left, on tree trunk
supporting crucifix; HIER - AMADI - AUG
- F -, on right, below the devotee
Acquisition: 1850, by legacy of
Felicita Renier
Last restored: 1948

Because of their different lettering it was
long doubted whether the signature,
which is certainly in the artist's hand, and
the inscription beneath the devotee were
contemporaneous. However, critics now
accept the reference to Girolamo as an
original one. The Amadi family came
from their native Lucca to settle in
Venice where they had the Church of
Santa Maria dei Miracoli erected. This
work, which the Reniers acquired in
1812, was therefore commissioned by a
Venetian, and, if not actually painted in
Venice, must have been there since its
very early years. It was probably executed in about 1450 after the artist's

stay in Ferrara. Moreover, there is
nothing Venetian in the landscape, whose
towers and turrets in the distant
background remind one of similar
features in della Francesca's *Baptism*,
now in London. The colour work of the
picture has deteriorated considerably: the
green used for the foliage of the tree and
in the landscape is a resinate of copper
which has turned to a burnt chestnut colour. The canvas has not been reduced
in size as is sometimes supposed. In the
stillness of a countryside contained within
two cylindrical shapes — both tree
trunks, on one of which is a crucifix —
the figures are spelt out with all their uns-
tained purity and deep absorption. "A
synthetised perspective of colour, form
and light", a characteristic which was to
be fundamental to Giovanni Bellini, as
indeed to all Venetian painting now well
on the way towards its exquisitely coloured symbolic view of life.

Bibliography: S.M.M., 1955, pp.
174-175, n. 196; P. De Vecchi, 1967,
p. 86.

Piombo, del, Sebastiano
see Luciani, Sebastiano

Pitati, de', Bonifacio
(Bonifacio Veronese)
Verona 1487 - Venice 1553

209. *The Madonna of the Tailors*
Oil on canvas, 130 × 149 cm
(cat. n. 1305)
Inscription: MDXXXIII / A DI VIIII / NOVĒB,
on base at centre; BONIF/ACIO. F., set
back, on step
Acquisition: 1945, from the Royal
Palace, Venice

This picture, which was originally in the Tailors' School near to the Church of the Jesuits, is the first work to be signed by Bonifacio de' Pitati and is dated 1533. A disciple of Palma il Vecchio, the artist shows all the signs of being influenced by manneristic ideas in the studied delicacy with which he has treated the figures, especially the saint and the beggar.

Bibliography: S.M.M., 1962, pp. 31-32, n. 55; S. Simonetti, 1983, p. 152.

210. *The rich epicure*
Oil on canvas, 204 × 436 cm
(cat. n. 291)
Acquisition: 1812, by purchase from the Grimani family of Venice

Recorded by Boschini in 1660 as being in the house of Procurator Giustiniani, this picture is known to have been in the Grimani Palace, Venice, in 1763. It is undoubtedly a Bonifacio de' Pitati masterpiece and fascinates us more than anything else for the intensity of the story it tells. Its tonal values and delicacy of touch are truly neo-Byzantine, blending as they do in an uninterrupted succession of charming observations on Nature and the customs of the time. The central group seems to be carried away by music, the ragged beggar solicits alms, hunters rest, lovers emerge from the woods. An idyllic peace reigns over the portico of a sumptuous villa and no one seems to notice the fire which rages furiously against the skyline to the right.

Bibliography: S.M.M., 1962, p. 35, n. 60.

211. *The Announcing Angel*
Oil on canvas, 196 × 134 cm
(cat. n. 942)
Acquisition: 1919, following the suppression edicts
Last restored: 1963

Together with the two canvases which follow, this painting, which occupied the left-hand side of a single picture dates from a little after 1540 when it was hanging in the Palazzo dei Camerlenghi, the seat of the Exchequer in Venice. It was divided into three sections after 1808. As a triptych, it was one of the very many canvases painted by Bonifacio Veronese and his assistants (1529-1545) to adorn the finance offices in the Palazzo, which was built near the Rialto Bridge between 1525 and 1528 under Doge Andrea Gritti.

Bibliography: S.M.M., 1962, pp. 46-47, n. 73; G.T. Faggin, 1963, p. 92 *et seq.*.

212. *Our Lady of the Annunciation*
Oil on canvas, 196 × 136 cm
(cat. n. 943)
Acquisition: 1919, following the
suppression edicts
Last restored: 1963

The right-hand section of the picture,
which has for its centrepiece *The Eternal Father and St. Mark's Square* (see
n. 213) is, like the above, expressed with
great feeling in a fine, easy-flowing style.

Bibliography: S.M.M., 1962, pp. 46-47,
n. 73; G.T. Faggin, 1963, p. 92 *et seq.*

213. *The Eternal Father and St.
Mark's Square*
Oil on canvas, 188 × 132 cm
(cat. n. 917)
Acquisition: 1919, following the
suppression edicts

This is the central section of the painting which includes *The Announcing Angel*
(see n. 211) and *The Virgin Mary* (n.
212). The three panels, which adorned
the Magistracy of the Camera degli Imprestidi (loans) in the Palazzo dei
Camerlenghi, were taken to Vienna in
1816 and were not returned until 1919.
In this bird's eye view we see St. Mark's
Square with the Basilica, the Ducal
Palace, the Piazzetta with its two columns, the Island of St. George and Basin,
part of the Giudecca, the Campanile and
old buildings around it, also the Loggetta. As Sansovino completed the Loggetta in 1540 the painting must be slightly
later than this date.

Bibliography: S.M.M., 1962, p. 46, n.
73.

Pittoni, Giambattista
Venice 1687-1767

214. *Crassus sacks the Temple of
Jerusalem*
Oil on canvas, 55 × 73 cm
(cat. n. 741)
Acquisition: 1910, by purchase from
the Milani family of Verona
Last restored: 1961

Sources record that this picture was once
in Conte Algarotti's Gallery in Venice,
that it passed into the collection of Belloni
Corniani Algarotti of Padua and then to

the Milanis of Verona. It is the model of
a painting commissioned in 1743 by
Francesco Algarotti for the Augustus III
Art Gallery in Dresden and finished by
Pittoni before 24 February 1744. The
lively scene is lit by an intensive play of
light and shade applied with great skill
and fine preciosity.

Bibliography: S.M.M., 1970, pp. 78-80,
n. 169; F. Žava Boccazzi, 1979, p. 172,
n. 213.

215. *Mary Magdalene*
Oil on canvas, 47 × 38 cm
(cat. n. 707)
Acquisition: 1903, by gift of W. Bode

A preliminary work dating from before
1740 for a larger altarpiece once in the
Church of Santa Maria Maddalena in
Parma and now in the Art Gallery of that
city. This small canvas is all the more expressive inasmuch as the supple flow of
the original concept loses its liveliness in
the treatment of the larger picture.

Bibliography: S.M.M., 1970, p. 80, n.
170; F. Žava Boccazzi, 1979, p. 172,
n. 212.

216. *The Annunciation*
Oil on canvas, 153 × 205 cm
(cat. n. 438)
Acquisition: 1807, from the Old Academy of Venice
Last restored: 1961

Painted in 1757 and displayed after the death of the artist at the Ascension Day Fair of 1777, this picture was Pittoni's contribution to the adornment of the Assembly Hall of the Academy at Fon-

teghetto della Farina for which Angeli (see entry n. 5) and Marinetti (see n. 170) had also worked. The artist clearly shows that his interest had by now turned to formal compositions executed in a style modelled on an increasing aptitude for virtuosity.

Bibliography: S.M.M., 1970, pp. 80-81, n. 171; F. Zava Boccazzi, 1979, p. 172, n. 214.

Ponte, da, Jacopo
(Bassano, Jacopo)
Bassano 1517-1592

217. *Adoration of the Shepherds*
Oil on canvas, 95 × 140 cm
(cat. n. 1360)
Acquisition: 1983, by purchase from Conte Justo Giusti del Giardino

A work on the same subject is recorded as being in the Giusti del Giardino family in 1620, and this may be the one. It appears to date from the mid-1540s and would therefore have been painted at about the same time as his *Flight into Egypt* now in the North Simon Museum

of Art in Pasadena, and a little later than his *Adoration of the Shepherds* in Hampton Court. These works show how Bassano combined descriptive qualities of the highest order tempered by the manneristic example of Parmigianino. Nor is his power of realistic observation lacking in this picture. It is to be seen in the animals and, above all, in the faces of the shepherds which are true portraits of humble folk.

Bibliography: L. Magagnato, 1981, p. 171, n. 53; R. Pallucchini, 1982, p. 28.

218. *St. Jerome*
Oil on canvas, 119 × 154 cm
(cat. n. 652)
Acquisition: 1900, by purchase from Alessandro Bedendo of Mestre

Almost certainly the same picture that Ridolfi mentioned in 1648 as hanging in the Palazzo Widmann in Venice, it dates from the seventh decade of the previous century. By that time Jacopo Bassano had broken free from an exacting manneristic

preference for plastic relief and overworked tokens and come out for the naturalism of real life observation. And so in the cold evening light the Saint and his symbols of the hermit's life — a skull, books bound in rough leather, a crucifix tied to a tree trunk, an hour-glass — are evoked with amazing intensity in which the most haunting part is played by the colours.

Bibliography: S.M.M., 1962, p. 10, n. 10.

219. *St. Eleutherius blesses the devout*
Oil on canvas, 280 × 174 cm
(cat. n. 401)
Acquisition: 1829, following the suppression edicts
Last restored: 1829

Painted at the request of the School of the Mazzari to adorn the high altar of their Church of St. Eleutherius at Vicenza. Even though this picture was approved by Borghini in 1584 as attributable to Jacopo Bassano, the response of critics has not been wholehearted. While its colour may indeed lack the vitality of Jacopo's creative brush, the impression left is that it is of his inspiration executed in great part by his assistants at the beginning of the 1570s.

Bibliography: S.M.M., 1962, p. 11, n. 11.

220. *Rest on the Flight into Egypt*
Oil on canvas, 52 × 102 cm
(cat. n. 410)
Acquisition: 1838, by gift of Girolamo Contarini

A picture which has also been attributed to Francesco Bassano but is now thought to be a late work by Jacopo Bassano and his workshop.

Bibliography: S.M.M., 1962, p. 13, n. 13.

Ponte, da, Jacopo
(from his workshop)

221. *Landscape with shepherds and the burning bush*
Oil on canvas, 45 × 114 cm
(cat. n. 415)
Acquisition: 1838, by gift of Girolamo Contarini

Once attributed to Jacopo Bassano, this spreading landscape with the shepherd and his flock in the foreground, right, and in the left background the burning bush in which God revealed himself to Moses is today widely ascribed to that artist's workshop. It is seen as deriving perhaps from models by Francesco Bassano.

Bibliography: S.M.M., 1962, p. 25, n. 38.

153

Ponte, da, Leandro
(Bassano, Leandro)
Bassano 1557-1622

222. *The Raising of Lazarus*
Oil on canvas, 410 × 238 cm
(cat. n. 252)
Inscription: LEANDER / BASSANE IS / F
Acquisition: 1815, following suppression edicts
Last restored: 1981

Removed during the Napoleonic sequestrations from the Venetian Church of Santa Maria della Carità to the altar in the Mocenigo Palace, this large canvas was taken to Paris in 1797 and returned to Venice in 1815. Usually dated at the turn of the 16th century, the picture shows how the ideas and graphic brushwork of Jacopo Bassano crystallised into a humdrum but dignified combination of inventiveness and colour-work in the painting of his son Leandro.

Bibliography: S.M.M., 1962, p. 15, n. 16.

Ponte, da, Leandro
(attributed to)

223. *Portrait of a man*
Oil on canvas, 61 × 55 cm
(cat. n. 403)
Acquisition: 1838, by gift of Girolamo Contarini
Last restored: 1903

Yet another attribution to Jacopo Bassano, but in this case it would be more plausible to ascribe the portrait to his son Leandro, even though it is marked by the generic characteristics of the father in its stylistic features.

Bibliography: S.M.M., 1962, p. 19, n. 23.

Pordenone, Giovanni Antonio
see Sacchis, de', Giovanni
Antonio

Preti, Mattia
Taverna 1613-1699

224. *Homer*
Oil on canvas, 102 × 81 cm
(cat. n. 59)
Acquisition: 1821, by purchase from
the Abbot Parisi
Last restored: 1963

Acquired by the Academy as a work fathered by Caravaggio, this picture was later attributed to Pier Francesco Mola. Today general opinion assigns it to a youthful stage in the long career of Mattia Preti.

Bibliography: S.M.M., 1970, p. 146, n. 324.

Previtali, Andrea
Barbenno, Bergamo 1470/1480 - Bergamo 1528

225. *The Crib*
Oil on canvas, 133 × 215 cm
(cat. n. 639)
Acquisition: 1897, from the Church
of the Redeemer, by exchange
Last restored: 1982

Probably displayed originally in the Ducal Palace, this and the following painting are of a date between 1515 and 1525. Previtali was then improving his early formation by studying the works of the Bellinis and Lorenzo Lotto, both of which he much admired. Here we see him in a vein of unadorned realism softened by rustic charm.

Bibliography: S.M.M., 1962, p. 179, n. 296; P. Zampetti - J. Chiappini, 1975, p. 140.

226. *The Crucifixion*
Oil on canvas, 133 × 215 cm
(cat. n. 640)
Acquisition: 1897, from the Church
of the Redeemer, by exchange
Last restored: 1982

As in its companion piece (see previous entry) Previtali places the characters present at the *Crucifixion* in a wide setting which seems to catch an echo from the landscape of Giorgione and his school.

Bibliography: S.M.M., 1962, p. 179, n. 257; P. Zampetti - J. Chiappini, 1975, p. 141.

Quirizio da Murano
active between 1461 and 1478

227. *The Redeemer and a nun*
Panel, 114 × 87 cm (cat. n. 659)
Inscription: QUIRICIUS DE MURAN — F.,
at base on plinth of throne step with
the signature on a label. The angels'
scrolls bear writings that allude to the
Eucharist
Acquisition: 1901, by purchase
Last restored: 1979

Originally in the Convent of Santa Chiara
at Murano, having almost certainly been
commissioned by one of the nuns, this
panel was acquired by the Abbot Domenico Mastellini who left it to the engraver
G.M. Sasso. He reproduced it in about
1780, after which it passed into the San-
quirico and Guggenheim collections, and
finally to A. Marcato. It has been severely
damaged in areas of the landscape and
of the hands of the Saviour, who is seated
on a throne of the Lombard style. This
Muranese artist was a keen populariser
of the new Paduan trends and of Mantegna's style. The picture is thought to be
one of his later works.

Bibliography: S.M.M., 1955, p. 148, n.
161.

155

Quirizio da Murano (?)

228. *Madonna and Child*
Scalloped panel, 53 × 32 cm
(cat. n. 616)
Acquisition: 1812, following the
suppression edicts
Last restored: 1979

This panel, which was once in the Santa Croce Monastery in Venice, has been
the subject of a vast number of attributions. In the last catalogue it was assigned
to a follower of Bartolomeo Vivarini, but
it is now thought to have been painted
by Quirizio at a time when Vivarini's influence was at its height, as it appears
to have been when the *Madonna adoring the sleeping Child* (cat. n. 29), now
in these Galleries, was being painted. A
rather similar version exists in the
Cathedral of Trani.

Bibliography: S.M.M., 1955, pp.
162-163, n. 163; G. Gamulin, 1963, p.
18.

Ricci, Marco
Belluno 1676 - Venice 1730

229. *Landscape with women washing
clothes*
Oil on canvas, 136 × 198 cm
(cat. n. 457)
Acquisition: 1878, by purchase from
Count Zanetti of Venice
Last restored: 1963

This and the following landscape, which
both date from about 1720, are recorded
as being in the Corniani Algarotti Gallery
at Treviso, whence they passed by in-
heritance to Countess Perazzolo. Of fundamental importance in Marco Ricci's
listed works, they are happy reminders
of the artist's style when he is moved to
heroic or romantic visions inspired by Tiziano's designs and the engravings of
Domenico Campagnola in order to set
down some simple observation that is full
of life and true to Nature.

Bibliography: S.M.M., 1970, p. 85, n.
182.

230. *Landscape with horses and a drinking trough*
Oil on canvas, 136 × 197 cm
(cat. n. 456)
Acquisition: 1878, by purchase from Count Zanetti of Venice
Last restored: 1963

As in the splendid landscape above, here we have another fine re-evocation of Marco Ricci's native valleys where light plays the major part in creating effects of intense veracity. Such pictures the young Canaletto certainly looked deeply into.

Bibliography: S.M.M., 1970, p. 85, n. 181.

231. *Landscape with woodcutters*
Tempera on kidskin, 31 × 46 cm
(cat. n. 1308)
Acquisition: 1956, from the Royal Palace, Venice

A characteristic example of the last phase of Marco Ricci's active life during which he mastered the technique of painting in tempera on kidskin in order to produce particular effects of light and atmosphere.

Bibliography: S.M.M., 1970, p. 85 *et seq.*, n. 183.

232. *A Park and Country House*
Tempera on kidskin, 30 × 46 cm
(cat. n. 1307)
Acquisition: 1956, from the Royal Palace, Venice

Marco Ricci recaptures something of the everyday life of a patrician villa of mainland Veneto with the natural freshness of an observant eye.

Bibliography: S.M.M., 1970, p. 85 *et seq.*, n. 184.

Ricci, Marco
(his circle)

233. *The Waterfalls*
Oil on canvas, 139 × 111 cm
(cat. n. 454)
Acquisition: 1838, following the suppression edicts
Last restored: 1963

Attributed to Marco Ricci, even by recent critics, this picture must, however, be assigned, together with its companion piece in these Galleries (cat. n. 372), to a follower of the Bellunese artist. Its painter shows the qualities of a truly painstaking and diligent landscapist in works of this genre.

Bibliography: S.M.M., 1970, p. 86, n. 185.

Ricci, Sebastiano

Belluno 1660 - Venice 1734

234. *The Dream of Aesculapius*
Oil on canvas, 80 × 98 cm
(cat. n. 910)
Acquisition: 1929, by gift of
Alessandro Contini of Florence

In the early 18th century Sebastiano Ricci was well thought of in the important art centres of Europe, in London where he stayed from 1712 to 1716 and in Paris (1716). For the maturity of its Rococo style this little picture is placed in that same decade. With the greatest precision and self-assurance the artist weaves together every detail of the composition with quick, sure strokes, almost as in a lively ballet. Aesculapius, who descends from a cloud is, of course, instantly recognisable to the dreaming sleepers by his staff and serpent.

Bibliography: S.M.M., 1970, p. 87, n. 187; J. Daniels, 1976, p. 120, n. 348.

157

Robusti, Domenico
(Tintoretto, Domenico)

Venice 1560-1635

235. *The Dream of St. Mark*
Oil on canvas, 393 × 317 cm
(cat. n. 875)
Acquisition: 1924, from the Church of Santa Maria degli Angeli at Murano
Last restored: 1965

Originally on one side of the altar in a chapel of the Big Hall of the Scuola Grande di San Marco, this was one of the paintings which in 1585 Jacopo Tintoretto undertook to let the Brethren have providing they agreed to accept his son Domenico, a son-in-law and two friends as members of their Confraternity. After becoming State property by Napoleonic decree it passed in 1817 to the new Seminary della Salute and then to the Church of Santa Maria degli Angeli. The charming device of an angel appearing to the sleeping St. Mark and greeting him with the words "Peace be with you Mark, my Evangelist" is attributed to Jacopo Tintoretto but was certainly executed by his son Domenico.

Bibliography: S.M.M., 1962, p. 244, n. 420; R. Pallucchini - P. Rossi, 1983, p. 256.

236. *Portrait of Procurator Contarini*
Oil on canvas, 117 × 87 cm
(cat. n. 1012)
Inscription: Contarini coat of arms and the initials I.C., lower left corner
Acquisition: 1919, following the suppression edicts

Painted for the Citra Rooms of the Procuratorate in the Ducal Palace, this is a work of Domenico Tintoretto's maturity. It should therefore be of Giovanni Paolo Contarini who was elected Procurator in 1594 and died in 1604.

Bibliography: S.M.M., 1962, p. 216, n. 281.

237. *Portrait of a Senator*
Oil on canvas, 65×55 cm
(cat. n. 897)
Acquisition: 1919, following the
suppression edicts

This portrait of a senator of uncertain
identity has been ascribed to Jacopo
Bassano, to Jacopo Tintoretto and to his
son Domenico. The last of these attributions is now considered the most likely
one.

Bibliography: S.M.M., 1962, p. 243, n.
418; P. Rossi, 1973, p. 153.

Robusti, Jacopo
(Tintoretto, Jacopo)
Venice 1514-1594

238. *St. Mark frees a slave*
Oil on canvas, 415×541 cm
(cat. n. 42)
Inscription: JACOPO TENTOR F.
Acquisition: 1821, with other works
that were returned to Venice from
Paris
Last restored: 1965

The first of the canvases to be executed
by Jacopo Tintoretto for the Chapter Hall
of the Scuola Grande di San Marco, of
which in 1547 Marco Episcopi was Head
Guardian. This very large painting was
already finished in April 1548 since it was
in that month that Aretino wrote a letter praising Tintoretto on completion of
the work. The story of St. Mark mira-
culously saving the servant of a knight

from Provence who had abandoned his
master to venerate the relics of the saint
is the subject. It was an event that caused
a stupendous sensation in Venice at the
time. The tumultuous scene is stressed
by violent contrasts of chiaroscuro and
clashing tones of colours. The observer
has the feeling of being immediately
caught up in it as St. Mark plummets
down to free the victim.

Bibliography: S.M.M., 1962, p. 221, n.
394; R. Pallucchini - P. Rossi, 1982, p.
157, n. 132.

239. *Procurator Jacopo Soranzo*
Oil on canvas, 106×90 cm
(cat. n. 245)
Inscription: JACOBUS SUPERANTIO
MDX|X|II, at top
Acquisition: 1812, following the
suppression edicts
Last restored: 1957

When last restored it could be seen that
this portrait, which was originally in the
Supra Rooms of the Procuratorate in the
Ducal Palace, and in the past had been
attributed to Tiziano, was in fact a section of a much larger picture which
without the least doubt was the work of
Tintoretto. It was painted in about 1550,

in any case shortly before the death of
Soranzo in 1551. Along with another,
which is in the Sforza Castle in Milan,
it is a fine example of Tintoretto's skill
as a portraitist. His command of spon-
taneity and his ability to catch the expression of a subject brought out most
vividly the characters of those whom he
painted.

Bibliography: S.M.M., 1962, p. 224, n.
396; P. Rossi, 1973, p. 124.

240. *Creation of the Animals*
Oil on canvas, 140×196 cm
(cat. n. 900)
Acquisition: 1928, from the State
deposits of the Ducal Palace
Last restored: 1967

This and the two pictures described
below date from 1550. They were part
of the adornment started by Francesco
Torbido in the Hall of the Scuola della
Trinità in Venice. In the 16th century,
when the School was demolished to make

way for the Basilica della Salute, the three
canvases were transferred to the School's
new premises. The creation of the
animals is evoked with the finest precision: as if released from the Eternal
Father's bow the birds streak across the
sky while phosphorescent fish furrow the
waters. Behind the Creator a host of
creatures press forward, hardly able to
wait to be called to their new destiny.

Bibliography: S.M.M., 1962, p. 226, n.
399; R. Pallucchini - P. Rossi, 1982, p.
171, n. 149.

241. *Adam and Eve*
Oil on canvas, 150 × 220 cm
(cat. n. 48)

Acquisition: 1812, following the suppression edicts

Last restored: 1967

This painting for the Scuola della Trinità (see ns. 240 and 242) once shared a place of honour with two others, the *Creation of Adam and Eve*, now lost, and *The Forbidden Fruit*, part of which survives in the Uffizi Galleries in Florence. Adam and Eve are depicted here in a wooded arbour at a moment of suspense before committing the original sin. Away in the distance they can be seen, already in flight, chased from Eden by the angel with the flaming sword in the direction of unknown and inhospitable territories.

Bibliography: S.M.M., 1962, p. 225, n. 399; R. Pallucchini - P. Rossi, 1982, p. 161, n. 149.

159

242. *Cain and Abel*
Oil on canvas, 140 × 196 cm
(cat. n. 41)

Acquisition: 1812, following the suppression edicts

Last restored: 1977

When painting this last canvas for the decoration of the Scuola della Trinità (see ns. 240 and 241) Tintoretto perhaps had in mind Tiziano's version of the same subject painted for the ceiling of the Church of Santo Spirito in Isola and now in the sacristy of the Basilica della Salute. As in the first of the series (see n. 240), this bloodthirsty scene is treated with fresh and spontaneous artistic verve.

Bibliography: S.M.M., 1962, p. 225, n. 298; R. Pallucchini - P. Rossi, 1982, p. 172, n. 152.

243. *The Assumption of Our Lady*
Oil on canvas, 240 × 134 cm
(cat. n. 219)

Acquisition: 1814, following the suppression edicts

Last restored: 1955

Originally in the Venetian Church of San Stin (St. Stephen, priest), this painting is generally given a date in the early 1560s. With a degree of skill that some would say is too calculated the crowded composition is dominated by the figure of the Virgin ascending to Heaven with a graceful rotary movement.

Bibliography: S.M.M., 1962, p. 223, n. 395; R. Pallucchini - P. Rossi, 1982, p. 159, n. 139.

244. *St. Jerome and St. Andrew*
Oil on canvas, 225 × 145 cm
(cat. n. 898)

Acquisition: 1937, from the Ducal Palace, Venice

Last restored: 1937

This, with the painting that follows it, once flanked the *Madonna with four Senators* in the Salt Magistracy at the Palazzo dei Camerlenghi. It was commissioned by Giorgio Venier and Alvise Foscarini, whose official duties as Salt Magistrates ended on 31 September 1551 and 1 May 1552 respectively. The two saints seem to tower on either side of the Cross, which is set obliquely, thus giving an impression of extraordinary depth to the picture.

Bibliography: S.M.M., 1962, p. 228, n. 400; R. Pallucchini - P. Rossi, 1982, p. 166, n. 163.

245. *St. Louis, St. George and the Princess*
Oil on canvas, 226 × 146 cm
(cat. n. 899)
Acquisition: 1937, from the Ducal Palace, Venice
Last restored: 1937

Commissioned for the Salt Magistracy (see n. 244) by Andrea Dandolo and Girolamo Bernardo on concluding their duties as Salt Magistrates, the first on 6 September 1552 and the second on 9 October. A few years afterwards, in 1557, Dolce accused Tintoretto of indiscretion for having painted "St. Margaret astride a serpent". But the master's intention was to portray the princess with stupendous effect writhing in the grip of symbolic bonds and with head turned towards her rescuer St. George, whose declamatory gestures are self-evident. Meanwhile St. Louis of Toulouse stands aloof in pensive reticence.

Bibliography: S.M.M., 1962, p. 228, n. 401; R. Pallucchini - P. Rossi, 1982, p. 165, n. 162.

246. *The Crucifixion*
Oil on canvas, 282 × 445 cm
(cat. n. 213)
Acquisition: 1891, from the Rosary School of St. John and St. Paul, Venice
Last restored: 1967

Originally in the School of the Santissimo Sacramento attached to the Venetian Church of San Severo, in 1793 it had already come into the possession of the Rosary School of St. John and St. Paul. The date most commonly given to this picture is 1554-1555, a time when Tintoretto showed himself to be under the spell of the new leader of Venetian pictorial imagery, Paolo Veronese, whose influence waxed through the early 1550s.

Bibliography: S.M.M., 1962, p. 231, n. 404; R. Pallucchini - P. Rossi, 1982, p. 168, n. 171.

247. *The Presentation of Jesus in the Temple*
Oil on canvas, 239 × 298 cm
(cat. n. 725)
Acquisition: 1906, from the Church of the Jesuits in Venice
Last restored: 1950

After the destruction of the Church of Santa Maria dei Crociferi, for which it had been painted, this picture passed to the sacristy of the Church of the Jesuits, then newly built. It dates from the second half of the 1550s.
The composition centres mainly on the foreground where the figures assume grandiose poses and typically manneristic attitudes. Any Veronesian intensity the colours may once have had — and this characteristic marked Tintoretto's work during the early years of the decade — is either lost or has faded.

Bibliography: S.M.M., 1962, p. 233, n. 406; R. Pallucchini - P. Rossi, 1982, p. 167, n. 168.

248. *The Madonna in glory, with saints*
Oil on canvas, 347 × 254 cm
(cat. n. 221)
Acquisition: 1812, following the suppression edicts
Last restored: 1959

Mentioned in sources as once on the first altar on the left in the Venetian Church of SS. Cosma and Damiano on the Giudecca, since destroyed, this picture is of the Virgin and Child with Cecilia and Marina below and Cosma and Damiano in the foreground. Generally associated with the last years of Tintoretto, it is now thought to have been painted in the late 1550s, suggested by the lively use of colour and the dynamism of the figures, seemingly so mobile and varying in their positions.

Bibliography: S.M.M., 1962, p. 241, n. 415; R. Pallucchini - P. Rossi, 1982, p. 169, n. 172.

249. *Deposition*
Oil on canvas, 227 × 294 cm
(cat. n. 217)

Acquisition: following the suppression
edicts

Once in the Venetian Chiesa dell'Umiltà,
no longer standing, this canvas dates
from about 1560, judging by the intensive lighting which sets it in the contemporary style of the *Probatica Piscina*
(Sheep Pool) in the Scuola Grande di San
Rocco. The figures are closely woven in
a jumble of chiaroscuro which produces
a moving and dramatic effect.

Bibliography: S.M.M., 1962, p. 232, n.
405; R. Pallucchini - P. Rossi, 1982, p.
180, n. 227.

250. *The Stealing of the Body of St.
Mark*
Oil on canvas, 398 × 315 cm
(cat. n. 831)

Acquisition: 1920, from the
Sansovino Hall of the Library of St.
Mark (*Biblioteca Nazionale Marciana*)

Last restored: 1959

This canvas, the one immediately below
and another, *The Finding of the Body of
St. Mark*, now in the Brera Gallery,
Milan, were painted between 1562 and
1566 for the Upper Hall of the Scuola
Grande di San Marco. They were paid
for by the Head Guardian, Tommaso
Rangone. As the second half of the century progressed Tintoretto's fantasies

became increasingly extravagant. Here,
almost projecting from the foreground,
the group carrying the stolen body is
shown in exceptionally high relief. A
storm breaks, as if by a miracle, and men
and buildings are illuminated by a
phosphorescent light, while fleeting
figures stand out against the towering
magnificence of the monumental construction in the background.

Bibliography: S.M.M., 1962, p. 234, n.
407; R. Pallucchini - P. Rossi, 1982, p.
183, n. 243.

251. *St. Mark saves a Saracen*
Oil on canvas, 398 × 337 cm
(cat. n. 832)

Acquisition: 1920, from the
Sansovino Hall of the Library of St.
Mark

Last restored: 1959

Together with the above picture it was
moved in 1807 from the Scuola di San
Marco into the Ducal Palace and then,
in 1815, into the Library of St. Mark.
It shows the miraculous rescue by St.
Mark of a Saracen who invoked the saint
at the height of a storm. Again in this
canvas Tintoretto applies his flair for the
dramatic by recording a prodigious event
with amazing readiness and by the expressive use of light as an illustrative
medium.

Bibliography: S.M.M., 1962, p. 235, n.
408; R. Pallucchini - P. Rossi, 1982, p.
185, n. 245.

252. *Madonna and Child with SS.
Sebastian, Mark and Theodore,
venerated by three Camerlengos*
Oil on canvas, 221 × 521 cm
(cat. n. 210)

Inscription: UNANIMIS CONCORDIAE /
SIMBOLVS / 1566, at lower left

Acquisition: 1883, from the Church
of SS. John and Paul

Last restored: 1780-1781

Painted for the Magistracy of the City
Camerlengos in the Palazzo dei Camerlenghi in 1567, this vast canvas was
assigned to the Church of St. John and
St. Paul in 1817. It is a votive picture
in which the donors, Michele Pisani,
Lorenzo Dolfin and Marino Malipiero
can be identified. They are accompanied
by their secretaries with the money in a
sack. The composition is in the grandiose
manner but relaxed and well-measured

as the figures move over the two-colour
chessboard of a marble floor.

Bibliography: S.M.M., 1962, p. 238, n.
411; R. Pallucchini - P. Rossi, 1983, p.
193, n. 32.

253. *Doge Alvise Mocenigo*
Oil on canvas, 116 × 97 cm
(cat. n. 233)
Acquisition: from the Ducal Palace,
Venice
Last restored: 1959

Recorded in the Seicento as occupying
a place in the last room of the Procuratorate "de Ultra", the portrait dates
from between 1570 and 1577 when
Alvise Mocenigo was Doge.

Bibliography: S.M.M., 1962, p. 239, n.
412; P. Rossi, 1973, p. 125.

Romani, Girolamo
(Romanino)
Brescia 1484/1487 - c. 1566

254. *Deposition and saints*
Oil on panel, 183 × 185 cm
(cat. n. 737)
Inscription: HIERONYMI RU/MANI BRIXIANI
/ OPUS. M.D.X. MENSE DECEMBRI
Acquisition: 1909, by purchase from
the Marquis Strozzi Ridolfi of
Florence
Last restored: 1975

In this first signed and dated work, which
was painted for the old Church of San
Lorenzo in Brescia, Romanino shows his
marked affinity with the tonal qualities
of Tiziano. The colouring is lively and
intense, the composition animated yet
compact, and in this respect the painting foreshadows a romantic exuberance,
both "expressionistic" and anticlassical,
which was to become a dominant factor in the mature work of this Brescian
artist.

Bibliography: S.M.M., 1962, p. 180, n.
300; F. Valcanover, 1966, p. 163.

Rosso, Antonio
Tai, Pieve di Cadore c. 1450 - Mel
c. 1510

255. *Madonna and Child on throne,
with angels, symbols of the Evangelists
and SS. Michael and George* on the
capitals of the throne
Panel, 106 × 69 cm (cat. n. 644)
Inscription: OPUS ANTONIJ / RUBEI, on
pedestal of throne
Acquisition: 1899, by gift of M.
Guggenheim
Last restored: 1979

Originally in the oratory of the Zam-
berlani house in Pieve di Cadore, where
Lanzi saw it in 1809, this picture passed
through several hands — T. Jacobi at
Pieve di Cadore, Galeazzi at Valle di
Cadore, G. Cadorin in Venice — before
it was acquired by the M. Guggenheim
collection. Although late 19th and early
20th century criticism considered it to
be one of the artist's first works, the attempt to harmonise the perspective,
though still in a somewhat provincial style
of Gothic descent, points, rather, to the
artist's assimilation of the new Paduan
and Venetian trends. It is perhaps safer,
then, to place this picture at a slightly
later date in the 1470-1480 decade.

Bibliography: S.M.M., 1955, p. 149, n.
164; G. Dalla Vestra - D. De Paoli
Benedetti, 1975, pp. 45-46, 244.

Rusconi, Benedetto
(Diana)

Venice, records from 1482 - d. 9
February 1525

256. *Miracle of the Relic of the Holy Cross*
Canvas, 365 × 147 cm (cat. n. 562)
Acquisition: 1820, following the suppression edicts, exhibited in 1828
Last restored: 1958-1960

This picture, which has a large blank space on the right-hand side, was painted for the Sala dell'Albergo or Sala della Croce in the School of St. John the Evangelist (see entry n. 16). The subject has been variously interpreted by 17th and 18th century writers, but it refers to an episode which, according to the *Opuscolo dei Miracoli* of 1590, is said to have occurred on 10 March 1480. Under that date the four-year-old child of "Ser Alvise Finetti, scribe at the Camera degli Imprestidi (Office of Loan)", having fallen from an attic and being seriously injured was at once cured. The *Description* of paintings in the School's possession in 1787 associates this miracle with the picture. It is a work based on the most "modern" criteria of the new century

(16th), in particular on Lotto and Giorgione, and one which in the subtle play of light and shade gives a searching view of the inner courtyard and beyond. Painted in the first decade of the 1500s, it must be dated a little after 1502 when the Senate granted the School the right to accept fifty new members in order to raise funds for completing the decoration of their Albergo.

Bibliography: S.M.M., 1955, pp. 127-128, n. 130; V. Moschini, 1960, pp. 358-359; S. Mason Rinaldi, 1978, pp. 299-300; J.G. Bernasconi, 1981, p. 201.

163

257. *Madonna on throne with Child between SS. Jerome, Benedict, Mary Magdalene and Giustina*
Panel, 201 × 230 cm (cat. n. 82)
Inscription: BENEDICTUS / DIANE - PIX., at base in centre; another inscription on the right relates to the donor, Donna Fiordelisa, wife of Maestro Bertoli Bocaler
Acquisition: 1812, following the suppression edicts
Last restored: 1979

Probably painted for the Church of San Luca in Padua, this late work nonetheless reveals the same close link between the artist's early paintings and those of Lotto, complicated in this case by the influence of Boccaccino, during his second stay in Venice, in the rendering of the Madonna, and by certain Nordic and Lombard allusions which stem from Bartolomeo Veneto and Jacopo de' Barbari.

Bibliography: S.M.M., 1955, p. 126, n. 127; A. Paolucci, 1966, pp. 14-15.

258. *The Madonna, Child and St. John on throne between SS. Louis and Monica (or Anne)*
Panel, 181 × 152 cm (cat. n. 86)
Acquisition: 1832, when it was displayed in these Galleries having been acquired probably after the suppression edicts
Last restored: 1979

Originally over the sacristy altar in the Venetian Church of the Servites where it was surmounted by a lunette depicting the *Eternal Father*, possibly the same one that presided over Lorenzo Veneziano's great polyptych (see entry n. 151). In spite of some uncertainty by past critics, the panel is now firmly believed to be by the hand of Diana. It is modulated with grey and silver colour harmonies of rare delicacy with results not unlike those of a Romanino or a Moretto, and is pervaded by well assimilated reminders of Giorgione, but with deviations towards contemporary Friulian tastes in imagery. One of Diana's later works, it was probably painted in about 1520. In this picture St. Louis is almost a counterpart to his namesake in *St. Mark between St. Jerome and St. Louis* (Belfer collection, London), perhaps the painting that reminded Vasari of San Francesco della Vigna.

Bibliography: S.M.M., 1955, p. 128-129, n. 131; A. Paolucci, 1966, p. 17.

Sacchis, de', Giovanni Antonio (Pordenone)

Pordenone 1483/1484 - Ferrara 1539

259. *The Blessed Lorenzo Giustiniani and saints*
Oil on canvas, 420 × 220 cm

Inscription: JOANNIS / ANTONII / PORTUNA/ENSIS, on step at base

Acquisition: 1815, following the suppression edicts

Last restored: 1965

Originally over the altar of the Renier chapel in the Venetian Church of the Madonna dell'Orto, it was transferred to Paris in 1797, and restored to Venice in 1815. In 1532 Pordenone undertook to paint a large altarpiece for the Canons of San Giorgio in Algae who where known as the "turchini" Brothers on account of their deep blue habit, and who at the beginning of the 16th century officiated at the Church of the Madonna dell'Orto. The composition was to include the Blessed Lorenzo Giustiniani, two of the "turchini" Brothers, St. Augustine and St. Francis, St. Bernardin and St. John the Baptist. In its execution, Pordenone, with long experience in Venice and central Italy behind him, mellows the animation of the main figures and the intensity of the colour tones adopted in the 1520's, perhaps in deference to Parmigianino. But he remains faithful to the close-knit representation of the figures in a grandiose manner, as well as to the dramatic force of luminous effects. With this latter development he was soon to draw away from the aulic classicism of Tiziano to paint in that proto-manneristic style to which the young Jacopo Tintoretto was far from indifferent.

Bibliography: S.M.M., 1962, p. 174 *et seq.*, n. 287; F. Valcanover, 1966, p. 23; C. Furlan, 1984, p. 143.

Savoldo, Gian Girolamo

Brescia c. 1480 - c. 1550

260. *St. Anthony Abbot and St. Paul the Hermit*
Oil on panel, 165 × 137 cm (cat. n. 328)

Inscription: OPUS JOVAN...JERONIM / BRIXIA DE...ALDIS 1520 (?), fragmentary signature on stone at base in centre

Acquisition: 1856, by purchase from the Manfrin collection, Venice

Last restored: 1977

Recent restoration has brought to light the original signature of Savoldo and a date that seems to be 1520. A work which for its maturity in figurative and chromatic respects gave little support to the date of 1510, which was widely favoured by critics, can now be placed more solidly in the course of the Cinquecento. Following Lombard tradition the pictorial dialogue reflects the latest cultural innovation of the Tuscans, of Dürer, Giorgione and Leonardo. But the painting is basically founded on free and spontaneous observations of real life set down in rich and full colour lit by a terse light, as if subtly opening a pathway to the early work of Caravaggio.

Bibliography: S.M.M., 1962, p. 188, n. 316; F. Valcanover, 1984, pp. 27-29.

Schiavone, Andrea,
see Meldolla, Andrea

School of Brescia
First half of 16th Century

261. *The Nativity*
Oil on canvas, 85 × 75 cm
(cat. n. 1025)
Acquisition: 1938, from the Florence
Export Office to which it had been
presented in 1929 by Francis Jekyll

Attributed by some critics to Moretto, this
painting is certainly of the Brescian
School of the 1530s.

Bibliography: S.M.M., 1962, p. 147, n.
238.

School of Emilia (?)
Second half of 14th Century

262. *Triptych*
In central panel: *The Madonna of
Humility nurturing the Child*; in the
cyma at top: *The Crucifix between the
Virgin and St. John*. In the wings,
left: *St. John the Baptist*; right, *St.
Jerome*; above: *The Annunciation*.
Three panels, gold background, with
original cornice: central, 53 × 23 cm;
the wings, each 53 × 12 cm (cat. n.
2)
Acquisition: 1816, by legacy of
Girolamo Molin
Last restored: 1951

The oldest catalogues report the inscription ANTONIUS VEN...1368, today lost, but
almost certainly fictitious. At first exhibited without designation or reference
to a Venetian origin, this small portable
triptych was probably an object of adoration in the home. It is ascribed, though
with reservations, to the Emilian School,
possibly to Jacopino and Bartolomeo da
Reggio of whom no works survive other
than a polyptych which is now in the
Brera Art Gallery, Milan.

Bibliography: S.M.M., 1955, pp. 175-
176, n. 199.

School of Rimini
First half of 14th Century

263a-f. *The Kiss of Judas and Capture of Christ, Christ before Pilate, Christ mounting the Cross, The Crucifixion, Deposition and The Universal Judgement*
Six panels, gold background *graffito*: each 16 × 14 cm (cat. n. 26)
Acquisition: 1816, by legacy of Girolamo Molin
Last restored: 1979

These panels must have formed part of an altar-facing together with the five other *Scenes of Christ's Passion* in the Friedrich Museum in Berlin (n. 1110), perhaps, too, with a *Deposition* now in a private Roman collection.
Today, generally recognised by critics as belonging to the School of Rimini for their archaic interpretation of Giotto's work unified as an integrated group.

Bibliography: S.M.M., 1955, p. 177, n. 201.

Venetian School
Beginning of 15th Century

264. *The Arrival of the Magi*
Panel, 58 × 93 cm (cat. n. 12)
Inscription: fictitious signature of Guariento at base
Acquisition: 1816, by legacy from Girolamo Molin
Last restored: 1951

While conditional acceptance was given during the 19th century to the signature of this work — it was recognised as fictitious by Cavalcaselle in 1887 — the elegant stylised figures present, in fact, the clear mark and character of Gothic-International painting of a lively colouring that suggest that it is of Venetian origin.

Bibliography: S.M.M., 1955, pp. 32-33, n. 30. L. Cuppini, 1964, pp. 160-161.

Venetian School
Fourth decade of 16th Century

265. *Jesus among the Doctors*
Oil on panel, 152 × 176 cm (cat. n. 85)
Acquisition: 1816, by legacy from Girolamo Molin
Last restored: 1839

To either side of the doctors surrounding Christ stand St. Gregory and St. Jerome on the left, St. Augustine and St. Ambrose on the right. This panel, which at different times has been attributed to Pordenone, to Palma il Vecchio, to Girolamo Pennacchi and Pier Maria Pennacchi, also to Giovanni and Bernardino da Asola, certainly seems to be the painting of a mainland Venetian artist long versed in the work of Palma il Vecchio and of Pier Maria Pennacchi.

Bibliography: S.M.M., 1962, p. 194, n. 331; M. Lucco, 1978, p. 104.

Venetian-Byzantine School
14th and 15th Centuries

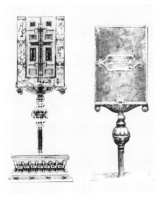

266. *The Reliquary of Cardinal Bessarione*
Wood, silver, gilded figures filigree, enamels, glass and precious stones. 47×32 cm (cat. n. S. 19)

Acquisition: 1919. With the suppression of the School of Santa Maria della Carità the Reliquary passed into the collection of Luigi Savorgnan, thence to the Abbot Luigi Celotti who sold it to the Emperor Francis I in 1821. Assigned to these Galleries with the Austrian restitutions made after the First World War

Donated to the School of Santa Maria della Carità in 1472 by Cardinal Bessarione, the famous scholar who by his legacy of manuscripts founded the Marciana Library. It is still kept at the School in the Sala dell'Albergo, where it was first placed, originally in a tabernacle painted by famous artists — one of them Gentile Bellini — but split up in the 18th century.
The Reliquary is in three parts: a gilded filigree Cross with a Christ figure in silver and green enamelled discs, beneath which a relic of the Holy Cross could be preserved, all mounted on a small panel, azure blue with gold stars, and set with four containers for relics, two small gilded plaques displaying the Archangels Gabriel and Michael, and the figures of Constantine and Helen painted on glass.
The casing consists of a fixed section framing the Reliquary on three sides with seven small scenes from the *Passion* and a loose shuttered cover presenting the *Crucifixion*. Behind the Reliquary a protective sheet of silver bears a plaque inscribed in Latin with a dedication to the School which Bessarione himself caused to be engraved. Other Greek inscriptions, controversial in their meaning, appear on the components, some of them having been transcribed in the Settecento when the Reliquary was disassembled. One of them refers to a certain "Irene Paleologina, daughter of the brother of the emperor" who would seem to have adorned the Cross in silver.
The work's origin, style and date are of highly uncertain origin and not only because the Princess Irene has not been identified but also because the mounting of the Cross and the painted casing probably date back to Bessarione. The casing has been variously ascribed to Byzantine-Palaeologue art of the second half of the Trecento, to the Italo-Cretan School, and finally with greater likelihood to craftsmen from Greece or Constantinople who were working in Venice in Bessarione's day.

Bibliography: S.M.M., 1955, pp. 191-194; L. Moretti, 1974, n. 112.

Venetian-Byzantine School
Beginning of 14th Century

267. *Madonna and Child*
Panel, 76×38 cm (cat. n. 884)

Acquisition: 1932, from Burano Cathedral

Last restored: 1939

This small panel, which is damaged round the sides, used to be in the Cathedral clergy house at Burano. It is much the same in style, form and attitude as the *Madonna nurturing the Child* now in the Marciano Museum. However, the marked Byzantine element with its stereotyped idiom would place it slightly later than the picture in the Marciano. It is probably of the very early 14th century.

Bibliography: S.M.M., 1955, pp. 17-18, n. 15; F. Zuliani, 1974, n. 76.

Venetian School (?)
End of 14th century

268. *The Madonna with Child and two devotees*
Panel, 188 × 138 cm

Inscription: MA/TER. / AVE. / XPI / SANC // TIBI / MA. VIRGO / MARIA / PARTU.., on the open book in the hand of the Virgin

Acquisition: received on deposit from the Church of Santa Caterina

The picture is damaged and there are some gaps. The clear influence of the Emilian School is to be seen in this serene rendering of the maternal condition, and not only in the confident human approach to the subject but also in the features of the small devout figures who probably represent the donors. Yet certain recognisable characteristics of Nicolò di Pietro's hand, together with the physical quality of the paintwork, lead one to suppose, however hesitantly, that the picture was executed by an artist of the Venetian School.

Bibliography: S.M.M., 1955, pp. 20-21, n. 19; R. Pallucchini, 1956, p. 71; A. Scarpa Sonino, 1975-1976, p. 783.

Venetian School
Second half of 14th Century

269. *Polyptych*
In central panel: *The Coronation of the Virgin*; in side panels: *Eight Stories of Christ: The Nativity, Christ among the Doctors, The Last Supper, Crucifixion, Deposition, Resurrection, Ascension, Pentecost*
Six panels, gold background: central, 55 × 39 cm; lateral, one with four *Stories*, 54 × 40 cm; the other four, each 26 × 19 cm (cat. n. 23)

Acquisition: 1816, by legacy of Girolamo Molin *The Coronation, Deposition, Resurrection, Ascension and Pentecost*. The panel with the four *Stories* belongs to the Correr Museum and was lent on deposit in 1954

Last restored: 1951-1954

These paintings making up a single polyptych of unknown origin were disassembled and remounted in 1957. Both groups comprising the *Stories of Christ* were once attributed to Simone da Cusighe owing to false inscriptions on *The Last Supper* and the *Deposition*. Nor is the signature of Semitecolo on the *Coronation* panel an original one. They were probably added when the polyptych was split up and one of the two groups of the *Stories* was divided into four small panels. An artist familiar with the style of Lorenzo Veneziano but mindful also of Catarino and of contemporaries working in Rimini is believed to be the author. A fragmentary triptych in the Correr Museum has also been closely compared with this polyptych and both works attributed to the so-called "Master of Christ Resurrected".

Bibliography: S.M.M., 1955, pp. 19-20, nn. 17-18; R. Pallucchini, 1964, pp. 213-214.

270. *Small portable altarpiece*
In central panel: *The Madonna of Humility*, with a *Pietà* in the cyme above; in the side panels: *SS. James and Francis*. On the back of the hinged panels depicting the two saints are shown the instruments of the Passion
Three panels, gold background: central, 119×75 cm; lateral, each 119×40 cm (cat. n. 14)
Acquisition: 1812, following the suppression edicts
Last restored: 1950

Originally in the Venetian Church of San Gregorio, this is one of the many small portable altarpieces made between 1370 and 1390 to standard iconographical compositions. Two such groups are to be distinguished and this one belongs to the earliest. Of good quality both in composition and in the clarity of its expressiveness, it is very much like the early work of Jacobello del Fiore and would therefore seem to date from about 1385.

Bibliography: S.M.M., 1955, pp. 18-19, n. 16; R. Pallucchini, 1964, p. 213.

Venetian School
15th Century

271. *Cross of St. Theodore*
Obverse: *Christ Crucified*, his blood being collected by flying angels. *Mary Magdalene* kneeling at foot of Cross; at sides: on interwoven leaves containing two medals symbolic of the School of St. Theodore, the *Virgin* and *St. John*. Reverse: *St. Theodore, Two kneeling Angels, Two half figures of Prophets*. Hexagonal knot: eight aedicules with the *Doctors of the Church* and the *Evangelists*. Rock crystal, silver in part gilded, 92×43 cm; bronze pedestal, height 46 cm (cat. n. S. 18)
Inscription: SCOLLA / DE - SANTO / TEODARO: 1567 - SOTO - IL - GUARDIANADO / DEL MA.ᶜᵒ MISIER - PIETRO - ROTTA / ET - COMPAGNI, on 16th century bronze triangular base
Acquisition: 1919. Following the Napoleonic requisitionings the Cross, like the *Reliquary of Cardinal Bessarione* (see entry n. 266), passed

into the collection of Count Savorgnan, thence to the Abbot Celotti who in 1821 sold it to the Austrian Emperor. It was assigned to these Galleries with restitutions made after the First World War

Once in the Scuola Grande di San Teodoro, this processional cross is of the same group as four other crosses existing in Venice. They were made for the Scuola di San Giorgio degli Schiavoni, the Scuola Grande di San Giovanni Evangelista and for Santo Spirito, the latter having been moved to Santa Maria della Salute. Of exquisite craftsmanship, erroneously attributed to the Da Sesto workshop, this Cross displays certain new features brought in by Tuscans working in Venice. At the same time it maintains its general Gothic character of Nordic origin.

Bibliography: S.M.M., 1955, pp. 194-195; M. Colusso, 1981, p. 35.

Venetian School
Second Half of 15th Century

272. *Triumphal Arch of Doge Nicolò Tron*
Canvas, 140×98 cm (cat. n. 53)
Inscription: OBSE - LEG - EST - AUG - R - P (Observare leges est augmentum Rei Publicae), on the architrave; P.C. (Paolo Corner), N.V. (N. Vitturi), and A.V. (Antonio Venier), beneath the coats of arms supported by three cherubs
Acquisition: 1890. Became State property and was kept in storerooms of the Ducal Palace until that date

Painted for the Cavatter Magistracy in the Ducal Palace, this picture can confidently be placed between 1471 and 1473 in which years Nicolò Tron held the office of Doge. It is less easy to identify the author, though the hallmark of the Paduan-Mantegna school is clearly recognisable. Attributed by Longhi to

Alvise Vivarini, it seems, instead, to show a much closer affinity to works like Squarcione's *Madonna* in Berlin (Dahlem), to that of Schiavone in the Sabauda Gallery, Turin, and then of Zoppo, once in the Manfrin and then in the Wimborne collections. Some indeed have said that it is by Zoppo. This uncertainty need not, however, surprise one as it is obvious that a number of artists in contact with Squarcione reproduced prototypes taken from the Master's drawings. A more specific connection is to be seen with *The Dogal Oath of Cristoforo Moro* in the British Museum, London, a work known to be by Leonardo Bellini. And, in fact, the present painting has been attributed to Bellini's workshop.

Bibliography: S.M.M., 1955, pp. 151-152, n. 167; R. Longhi, 1969, p. 40; S. Steer, 1982, p. 193; A. De Nicolò Salmazo, 1983, p. 249.

Venetian School
End of 15th Century

273a. *Kneeling Angel with thurible*
Granular marble, height 100 cm
(cat. n. S. 8)

273b. *Kneeling Angel with incense-boat*
Granular marble, height 104 cm
(cat. n. S. 9)

273c. *Kneeling Angel with candlestick*
Granular marble, height 106 cm
(cat. n. S. 10)

273d. *Kneeling Angel with candlestick*
Granular marble, height 98 cm
(cat. n. S. 11)

Acquisition: 1924, from the
Archaeological Museum of the Ducal
Palace

Last restored: 1980

The origin of these figures is not known.
They formed perhaps part of an altar or
a funereal monument. Believed to be the
works of a Venetian artist of the late
Quattrocento, they show signs of Pietro
Lombardo's influence and have, in fact,
been attributed to a Lombard artist.

Bibliography: S.M.M., 1955, p. 191, n.
215; G. Mariacher, 1959, p. 203.

Venetian School
16th Century

274. *The Doge Ziani meets Pope Alexander III at the Carità*
Oil on canvas, 185 × 234 cm
(cat. n. 654)

Acquisition: 1884, from the Ducal
Palace, Venice

According to legend Pope Alexander III
took refuge in Venice from the invasion
of Barbarossa. The picture shows him
meeting the Doge of that day, Sebastiano
Ziani, 1172, outside the Church of Santa
Maria della Carità where it was perhaps
first hung. By an anonymous late Cinquecento artist, this is certainly the copy
of a larger canvas of a style close to that
of Gentile Bellini, and is important
because it shows us how the vanished
Gothic façades of the Church and Scuola
of Santa Maria della Carità looked at the
time.
In the church façade is portrayed a
lunette by Bartolomeo Bon and his
workshop now preserved in the right-
hand sacristy of the Basilica della Salute.

Bibliography: S.M.M., 1962, p. 206, n.
36.

Venetian School
Beginning of 16th Century

275. *Visitation*
Oil on canvas, 212 × 150 cm
(cat. n. 95)
Acquisition: 1814, following the suppression edicts
Last restored: 1955

It seems that this picture was originally painted for the Monastery of Sant'Andrea. Again, there have been various attributions: Tiziano, Sebastiano del Piombo, Cariani, Palma il Vecchio, Giorgione himself — all have had their supporters. However, we do not think that any of these claims can be upheld, though the painting undoubtedly bears some marks of the style of Giorgione's followers, particularly of Sebastiano del Piombo, so far as the figures are concerned.

Bibliography: S.M.M., 1962, p. 198 *et seq.*, n. 342; M. Lucco, 1980, p. 95, n. 16.

Sebastiano del Piombo
see Luciani, Sebastiano

Solimena, Francesco
Nocera dei Pagani 1657 - Barra 1747

276. *Rebecca and Abraham's Servant*
Oil on canvas, 202 × 150 cm
(cat. n. 870)
Acquisition: 1920, by purchase from the former Muti Palace at San Cassiano, near Venice
Last restored: 1963-1964

This and the picture that follows it were painted in about 1710 for the Venetian house of the Baglioni family in Rio Marin. They moved in the mid-18th century to Palazzo Muti at San Cassiano. Both paintings are of some importance as illustrating the vigorous naturalism which Giambattista Piazzetta and Giambattista Tiepolo launched in Venice in the 1720s.

Bibliography: S.M.M., 1970, p. 152, n. 870.

277. *Jacob and Rachel*
Oil on canvas, 198 × 150 cm
(cat. n. 871)
Acquisition: 1920, by purchase from the former Muti Palace at San Cassiano, near Venice
Last restored: 1963-1964

Like the above, the relationship of the figures in this picture is worked with balance and elegance. Forms show up all the better for the dark, heavily inked background in strong plastic relief created by the skilled use of light.

Bibliography: S.M.M., 1970, p. 152, n. 871.

Stefano di Sant'Agnese

active between 1369 and 1385

278. *Coronation of the Virgin*
Panel, gold background, 71 × 54 cm
(cat. n. 21)
Inscription: M̄CCCLXXXI / STEFAN /
PLEBANUS / SCĒ AGNET / PINXIT , on
edges of last step beneath the throne.
Here the word *plebanus* means
"parishioner"
Acquisition: 1816, by legacy of
Girolamo Molin
Last restored: 1951

This panel recalls one of similar composition which Paolo Veneziano painted for his polyptych in the Church of Santa Chiara (see entry n. 198). So much so that until 1950, when Paolo's original panel was returned to Venice by the

Brera Gallery, Milan, it was used as a substitute. Nevertheless, we see here a strong Gothic emphasis, in turn influenced by the idiom of both Veneziano and Guariento. It is interesting to note the way the artist achieves an impression of space within so complex an arrangement of the perspective planes and brings it out by the use of contrasting colours. A work that is not without significance since it exemplifies the change of taste that gained a hold on Venetian painting in the last decades of the 14th century.

Bibliography: S.M.M., 1955, pp. 21-22, n. 21; R. Pallucchini, 1964, pp. 191-192.

Strozzi, Bernardo

Genoa 1581 - Venice 1644

279. *The Feast in the House of Simon*
Oil on canvas, 272 × 740 cm
(cat. n. 777)
Acquisition: 1911, by purchase from avv. Paolo Sartori of Vicenza
Last restored: 1981

The version of a theme which Strozzi painted several times, this picture can be dated to the last years of the artist's life in Genoa, that is to the second half of the 1630s. It is possible that it originally adorned the private chapel of a Genoese

mansion belonging to the Gorleri family.
Recent restoration confirms that the entire work was by Strozzi who, in this immense composition, shows what an imaginative and expressive master of colour he was and how he was able to give a Baroque note to the innovations of Caravaggio. He benefited much from the example of the Lombard artists Cerano and Procaccini, also from Pier Paolo Rubens himself.

Bibliography: S.M.M., 1970, p. 105, n. 231.

280. *St. Jerome*
Oil on canvas, 56 × 47 cm
(cat. n. 424)
Acquisition: 1838, by gift of Girolamo Contarini
Last restored: 1962

Another subject much favoured by Strozzi, this version of St. Jerome is usually regarded as representing the artist's work shortly after he came to live in Venice. It therefore dates to the early 1640s.

Bibliography: S.M.M., 1970, p. 106, n. 232.

281. *Portrait of a Procurator*
Oil on canvas, 227 × 147 cm
(cat. n. 1358)
Acquisition: 1981, by purchase from
the Curtis collection, Palazzo
Barbaro, Venice

It is thought by some that this portrait
is of Giovanni Grimani, son of Antonio,
also a procurator, painted to com-
memorate his appointment as Am-
bassador to Vienna in 1636. It is probably one of the last works that Strozzi
undertook in Venice where he had come
at the beginning of the 1630s to make,
with Fetti and Liss, a notable contribution towards reviving the artistic life of
the Serenissima. The Procurator is presented in a most lifelike manner, a stead-

fast and imposing figure draped in official
robes, dark red sashed by a broad golden
coloured stole. It was to this type of
ceremonial representation that the great
Venetian portraitists committed themselves, from Sebastiano Bombelli to
Ghislandi and, above all, Alessandro
Longhi (see entry n. 142).

Bibliography: L. Mortari, 1966, p. 183;
R. Pallucchini, 1981, p. 159.

173

Sustris, Lamberto
Amsterdam 1515/1516 - c. 1595

282. *Christ in bonds, with view of
Jerusalem*
Oil on panel, 63 × 80 cm
(cat. n. 268)
Acquisition: 1816, by legacy of
Girolamo Molin
Last restored: 1959

At first recorded by these Galleries as a
work of Schiavone, this panel is now attributed to Sustris whose view of the distant Jerusalem is typical of the work of
one who drew much on the example of
the Dutch master, Jan van Scorel.

Bibliography: S.M.M., 1962, p. 214, n.
378.

Tiepolo, Giambattista
Venice 1696 - Madrid 1770

283. *Allegory of Old Age and Death*
Oil on copper, 11.5 × 9 cm
(cat. n. 1342)
Acquisition: 1968, by gift of Antonio
Morassi

Among the very earliest works of Giambattista Tiepolo, this picture shows the
influence exerted on the artist in his form-
ative years by the dramatic style of
Piazzetta and of Bencovich. This is apparent in his use of heavy chiaroscuro
and of intensive and tormented effects
emphasised by plasticity.

Bibliography: S.M.M., 1970, p. 240, n.
589.

284. *Diana and Actaeon*
Oil on canvas, 100 × 135 cm
(cat. n. 440)
Acquisition: 1898, by purchase from
Count Francesco Agosti of Belluno

This and the three mythological scenes
below display unmistakable signs of the
style of the young Giambattista Tiepolo
in the first half of the 1720s. Together
they form a unique series in which the
great Venetian artist depicts tales taken
from Ovid's *Metamorphoses*. He has
clearly sought to lessen the severity of the
light and shade contrasts by introducing
more luminous tones than hitherto.

Bibliography: S.M.M., 1970, p. 107.

285. *The Abduction of Europa*
Oil on canvas, 100 × 135 cm
(cat. n. 435)

Acquisition: 1898, by purchase from
Count Francesco Agosti of Belluno

From his earliest years as a painter Giambattista Tiepolo always interpreted space in an open, freely flowing style. His settings, which recall the works of Pellegrini and Sebastiano Ricci, were bathed in light, thus giving emphasis to the delicacy and liveliness of the colours.

Bibliography: S.M.M., 1970, p. 107, n. 236.

174

286. *Diana discovers that Callisto is pregnant*
Oil on canvas, 100 × 135 cm
(cat. n. 712)

Acquisition: 1907, by purchase from
Countess Capponi of Belluno

This mythological scene is strictly faithful to Ovid. A light Rococo rhythm runs through the allegorical group and the colour and lighting effects that discreetly illuminate the episode.

Bibliography: S.M.M., 1970, p. 107, n. 235.

287. *Apollo and Marsyas*
Oil on canvas, 100 × 135 cm
(cat. n. 711)

Acquisition: 1907, by purchase from
Countess Capponi of Belluno

Even more effectively than in the mythological scenes shown above, the young Giambattista Tiepolo shows his ability to treat a subject with exceptional fluency by grouping the figures on different planes in an open spatial setting.

Bibliography: S.M.M., 1970, p. 107, n. 237.

288. *St. Dominic glorified*
Oil on canvas, 78 × 77 cm
(cat. n. 810)

Acquisition: 1922, by purchase from
Charles de Burlett of Berlin

This small canvas calls to mind Giambattista Piazzetta's stupendous rendering of the same subject painted in about 1726 for the ceiling of St. Dominic's Chapel in the church of St. John and St. Paul. The same amazing freshness of light and colour, the same creative approach to interpreting space as in Piazzetta's masterpiece are seen here in the much reduced form that Tiepolo adopted without in any way diminishing the lively fascination of the scene.

Bibliography: S.M.M., 1970, p. 108, n. 238; U. Ruggeri, 1983, p. 86 *et seq.*, n. 25.

289. *The Punishment of the Serpents*
"Thin" oils on canvas, 164 × 1356 cm
(cat. n. 343)
Acquisition: 1892, following
sequestration under the Napoleonic
edicts
Last restored: 1893

Painted towards the end of the 1720s for
the Church of SS. Cosma and Damiano
on the Giudecca, this frieze is exceptional
for its richness of invention. It is divided
into three main episodes which form an
uninterrupted sequence within false stucco cornices. The eloquent colour tones ac-
centuate the moving aspects of a story
which in effect is loaded with melodrama.
Bibliography: S.M.M., 1970, p. 110.

290. *St. Joseph with the Child Jesus
and SS. Francis of Paola, Anne,
Anthony and Peter of Alcantara*
Oil on canvas, 210 × 114 cm
(cat. n. 484)
Acquisition: 1838, following the
suppression edicts
Last restored: 1960-1961

A work dating from the first half of the
1730s when it was painted for a church
dedicated to San Prosdocimo which
belonged to the Benedictine nuns of
Padua. Something of Piazzetta's influence is apparent in the dark colour
tones and in the impressive structural arrangement of the composition.

Bibliography: S.M.M., 1970, p. 109, n.
240.

291. *The Holy Family appears to
San Gaetano*
Oil on canvas, 128 × 73 cm
(cat. n. 481)
Acquisition: 1887, by purchase from
the Königsberg Foundation for
Charity, Vienna

This picture, which once adorned the
altar of the chapel in Palazzo Labia,
Venice, was painted in 1735. With inspired fantasy Giambattista Tiepolo sets
the vision in the proximity of a church,
over which the Holy Family and San
Gaetano are poised in a celestial light
which reverberates through white clouds.

Bibliography: S.M.M., 1970, p. 110, n.
242.

292. *The Translation of the Holy
House of Loreto*
Oil on canvas, 124 × 85 cm
(cat. n. 911)
Acquisition: 1930, by purchase from
the heirs of the sculptor del Zotto

Two sketches of September 1743 are
known to exist for the huge oval-shaped
fresco which Tiepolo painted on the ceiling of the Scalzi church (see next entry).
One is in the Rosebery collection in
England, the other belongs to these
Galleries and is shown here. The artist's
ability to convey in so small an area the
idea of boundless space is truly fascinating. In doing so he scales his colour tones
into a symphony of amazing splendour
with notes perceptible from the remotest
distance.

Bibliography: S.M.M., 1970, p. 111, n.
243; W. Barcham, 1979, pp. 430-447.

293. *Devout persons looking down from a loggia*
Detached fresco, 400 × 198 cm
(cat. n. 836)
Acquisition: 1915, from the Church of Santa Maria of Nazareth, called "the Scalzi"
Last restored: 1916-1917

This fresco, and the one below (n. 294), formed part of a very large painted area of the ceiling of the "Chiesa degli Scalzi" which was almost wholly destroyed during the Austrian bombardment on the night of 24 October 1915.
As well as painting *The Translation of the Holy House of Loreto*, Tiepolo completed his splendid work on this church between November 1743 and November 1745 with the help of Girolamo Mengozzi Colonna who portrayed the false architectural effects. Of this feat in church interior decoration there remains little other than the mock loggia with its two devotees in prayer and a third staring sidelong down the nave. Against the silvery gleam of the sham architecture their clothes are shown in harmonies and contrasts that recall Paolo Veronese's skill in the use of colour tones.

Bibliography: S.M.M., 1970, p. 112, n. 244.

294. *Devout persons looking down from a loggia*
Detached fresco, 400 × 186 cm
(cat. n. 837)
Acquisition: 1915, from the Church of Santa Maria of Nazareth, called "the Scalzi"
Last restored: 1916-1917

As in the above, these contemporary figures show passionate devotion before the sacred rites. The close matching of the colour values adds greatly to the luminous quality of the scene.

Bibliography: S.M.M., 1970, p. 112, n. 245.

295. *The Exaltation of the Holy Cross*
Oil on canvas, 52 × 51 cm
(cat. n. 789)
Acquisition: 1913, by purchase from Generoso Añes of Toledo

The preliminary sketch for the painting in the Capuchin Church at Castello (see n. 296). A miniature draft which hints at the beauty of the boldly inventive concept of space and perspective, but not of the light which is raised to intensive brilliance in the larger tondo (below), also in these Galleries.

Bibliography: S.M.M., 1970, p. 112, n. 246.

296. *The Exaltation of the Holy Cross*
Oil on canvas, diameter 486 cm
(cat. n. 462)
Acquisition: 1812, following the suppression edicts
Last restored: 1982

Tiepolo's centrepiece to Girolamo Mengozzi Colonna's adornment of the ceiling of the Capuchin Church at Castello. Since its recent restoration one has been able to admire the intensity and splendour of the combined colour effects which, for their decorative elegance put this painting on a comparable footing with those executed for the ceiling of the Upper Hall in the Scuola del Carmine between 1743 and 1745.

Bibliography: S.M.M., 1970, p. 115, n. 250.

Tiepolo, Giandomenico
Venice 1727-1804

297. *Three angels appear to Abraham*
(cat. n. 834)
Acquisition: following the suppression edicts
Last restored: 1960

This was painted by Giandomenico after winning the competition announced in 1772 to finish the decoration of a room called "the new Chancellery" in the Scuola della Carità. A re-elaboration of the decorative paintings of his father, Giambattista, is suggested in the static figurative forms and in the use of a "more chalky" palette. By this time the artist was under the influence of the neo-classical movement.

Bibliography: S.M.M., 1970, p. 114.

Tintoretto, Domenico
see Robusti, Domenico

Tintoretto, Jacopo
see Robusti, Jacopo

Tiziano
see Vecellio, Tiziano

Traversi, Gaspare
Naples, records from 1749 to 1776

298. *The Wounded Man*
Oil on canvas, 100 × 127 cm
(cat. n. 1197)
Acquisition: 1956, by purchase from the Venice Export Office

Mentioned in 1888 as being in the collection first of Professor Licata and then of Duke Melito of Naples and Italico Brass of Venice, this picture provides ample proof of a revival in the early 1750s of those mental and emotional attitudes of which Gaspare Traversi availed himself to treat the realities of life with merciless objectivity.

Bibliography: S.M.M., 1970, p. 153, n. 348.

Trevisani, Angelo
Treviso (?) 1669 - 1753/1755

299. *Driving the merchants from the Temple*
Oil on canvas, 120 × 121 cm
(cat. n. 790)
Acquisition: 1912, by purchase from the antiquarian S. Candian
Last restored: 1960

This is the sketch, with notable variations, for an important painting which Angelo Trevisani executed in 1732 for the Venetian church of SS. Cosma and Damiano on the Giudecca. After the Napoleonic sequestrations it was removed to Milan and in 1818 was placed on deposit with the parish church at Somaglia, near Lodi.

Bibliography: S.M.M., 1970, p. 118, n. 254.

Tura, Cosmè

c. 1430 - Ferrara 1495

300. *Madonna and sleeping Child*, also called *The Madonna of the Zodiac*
Panel, 61 × 41 cm; original frame, 121 × 69 cm, including lunette of 19 × 56 cm (cat. n. 628)
Inscription: SVIGLIA EL TUO FIGLIO DOLCE MADRE PIA/PER FAR IN FIN FELICE L'ALMA MIA, on the parapet at base
Acquisition: 1896, by purchase from Sig.ri Coen Rocca-Luzzato of Venice
Last restored: 1892

This panel, once in the Bertoldi farmhouse at Merlara, near Padua, was probably a household treasure in the family for whom it was painted. Its frame is a contemporary one in the Donatello style, and on the tympanum appears the emblem of St. Bernardin supported by two angels.
Behind the Madonna to the left four Signs of the Zodiac are painted in gold: Aquarius, Pisces, Sagittarius and Virgo; traces of others are still visible in the background on the right. It is a work of the artist when young, and although recently compared with Tura's paintings of 1469 made for the organ-case of Ferrara Cathedral, it seems more likely that it dates from the same period as his *Primavera*, now in London, which can be placed between 1460 and 1463, as stated in the catalogue of 1955. The picture has a highly translucent quality obtained with the use of vitreous paints which give it almost material substance. And it does not show any trace of the formal sourness and haunted look that is common to later Ferrarese works. Tura's motif of the sleeping Child was to be repeated in detail in his mature Roverella polyptych.

Bibliography: S.M.M., 1955, pp. 179-180, n. 205; R. Molajoli, 1974, p. 84; M. Boskovits, 1978, p. 378.

Valentin de Boulogne

Coulommiers en Brien 1592 - Rome 1634

301. *The Martyrdom of St. Bartholomew*
Oil on canvas, 121 × 165 cm (cat. n. 62)
Acquisition: 1821, by purchase from the Abbot Parisi

At one time attributed to Mattia Preti as well as to Ribera, in the light of recent criticism this picture came in fact from the hand of the French artist Valentin de Boulogne, who was a disciple of Caravaggio.

Bibliography: S.M.M., 1970, p. 177, n. 415.

*Vecchia, della, Pietro
see Muttoni, Pietro*

302. *Presentation of the Virgin at the Temple*
Oil on canvas, 335 × 775 cm
(cat. n. 626)
Acquisition: remains on the wall for which it was painted
Last restored: 1981

This painting was finished by Tiziano in 1539 to cover one of the walls in the Sala dell'Albergo of the Scuola della Carità where it can be seen to this day. The blank space at the foot of the Temple steps on the right is authentic, the one on the left was made in Tiziano's lifetime. Tiziano's wonderful sense of classical col-

our tones reaches its highest peak of sensitivity in this stupendous picture. The tones blaze up in all parts of the vast composition and are richly matched in harmonies far from the sensuous intimacies of Giorgione's brush, while every figure fits into the natural context of rôle and epoch. While the spreading grandeur of a setting in which the slender girl is isolated within a celestial vesica may have been forced to the very limit of academic welcome, all other details are unforgettable for their chromatic brilliance.

Bibliography: S.M.M., 1962, p. 258, n. 451; G. Nepi Sciré, 1984, p. 151.

303. *St. John the Baptist*
Oil on canvas, 201 × 134 cm
(cat. n. 314)
Inscription: TICIANUS, on the stone upon which the Baptist is resting one foot
Acquisition: 1808, following the suppression edicts
Last restored: 1981

Originally over the altar of the chapel on the left side of the high altar in the Venetian church of Santa Maria Maggiore. After recent restoration, which brought to light the fullness of the colouring matter, the picture is now believed to date from the early 1540s if not from the last years of the previous decade. It shows

much evidence of Tiziano's desire to strengthen his naturalistic bent with mannerist elements. Thus, in his theatrical pose and unmistakably "michelangelesque" plasticity of form, the Baptist resembles more a muscular athlete who has just returned from an excursion into the mountains of Cadore than a hermit wizened by long fasts in the wilderness.

Bibliography: S.M.M., 1962, p. 259, n. 452; F. Valcanover, 1981, p. 100 *et seq.*, n. 15.

304. *Madonna and Child*
Oil on canvas, 124 × 96 cm
(cat. n. 1359)
Acquisition: 1981, by legacy of Leonardo Albertini

Recorded in the early 1600s as a recognised work of Tiziano's belonging to the Marquis Mazenta of Milan, this Madonna dates from the beginning of the 1560s. Current restoration will undoubtedly confirm its affinity with the signed *Madonna and Child* now in the Alte Pinakothek at Munich. The figures of the Virgin and Child are built up by impasting colours infused with light which fades to a glow in the burning bush in the top left corner. Recent reflectoscopic examination indicates that the work was executed on

a canvas already used for another subject, possibly the painting of a saint in prayer.

Bibliography: H.E. Wethey, 1969, I, p. 100, n. 52; *Riflettoscopia...*, 1984, pp. 34-41.

305. *Pietà*
Oil on canvas, 352 × 349 cm
(cat. n. 400)
Inscription: QUOD / TITIANUS INCHOATUM
RELIQUIT / PALMA REVERENTER
ABSOLUIT... DEOQ. DICAVIT OPUS, at base
in centre
Acquisition: 1814, following the
suppression edicts
Last restored: 1983-1984

Intended by Tiziano for this burial place
in a chapel at the Frari, this *Pietà* is
recorded in the Seicento as being in the
Venetian Church of Sant'Angelo, since
demolished. It was left unfinished at the
death of the artist. Restoration work on
the picture, 1983-1984, definitely confirms that the figural part in the
foreground was painted over another
composition. It also shows that Palma il
Giovane's completion of the work after
Tiziano's death was limited to the angel
with the torch and to touching up the
tympanum of the stone shrine. The opa-

que density of these features contrasts
with the "magic impressionism" (R.
Longhi) of Tiziano's palette which in his
last days on earth showed signs of a
cosmic sense of the tragic in the way he
pushed "chromatic alchemy" to the limits
of expressiveness. In the glow of the ap-
sidal shell the human passions are illustrated in diagonal descent. And, as in
the mosaic work of the shrine over which
funereal oil lamps burn, the two figures
of Moses and the Hellespont Sibyl almost
seem to melt in a warm glow of golden
light. Above the votive plaque and the
leonine bust, and close to the dress of the
Sibyl, the artist painted a hand open in
a beseeching manner. Was it to ward off
his approaching death and that of his
favourite son, Orazio, who died soon
after the father?

Bibliography: S.M.M., 1962, p. 260, n.
453; G. Nepi Sciré, 1985.

Vecellio, Tiziano
(his workshop)

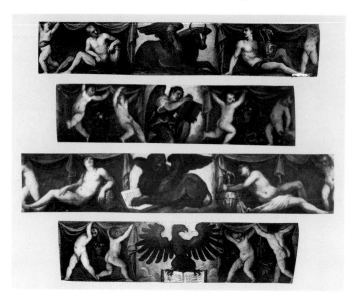

306a. *Symbol of St. Luke the
Evangelist: a bull*
Oil on canvas, 46 × 236 cm
(cat. n. 454a)
306b. *Symbol of St. Matthew the
Evangelist: an angel*
Oil on panel, 49 × 202 cm
(cat. n. 454b)

306c. *Symbol of St. Mark the
Evangelist: a lion*
Oil on panel, 45 × 240 cm
(cat. n. 454c)

306d. *Symbol of St. John the
Evangelist: an eagle*
Oil on panel, 49 × 198 cm
(cat. n. 454d)

Acquisition: 1812, following the
suppression edicts

Last restored: 1935

Together with other panels displaying
masks and chiaroscuro heads, these four
adorned the ceiling of the "Albergo" of
the Scuola di San Giovanni Evangelista
in Venice. At their centre was *The Vision of St. John in Patmos*, which is now
in the Washington National Gallery.
Although not authentic Titianesque work,
the four panels shown here come from
the Vecellio workshop which designed
the painting of the ceiling between 1544
and 1548.

Bibliography: S.M.M., 1962, p. 262, n.
454; H.E. Wethey, 1969, p. 138, n.
112.

Vecellio, Tiziano
(a follower of)

307. *The Archangel Raphael and Tobiolo*
Oil on canvas, 170 × 146 cm
(cat. n. 1325)
Inscription: the Bembo coat of arms towards centre of base
Acquisition: following the suppression edicts
Last restored: 1956

Originally in the Venetian church of Santa Caterina, this painting passed with the building into State hands at the time of the Napoleonic decrees. It has been attributed to Tiziano, to Sante Zago and to Paris Bordone. Recent critics are, however, agreed that the author of the panel is a follower of the youthful Tiziano.

Bibliography: S.M.M., 1962, p. 264, n. 458; H.E. Wethey, 1969, I, p. 179, n. 39.

Veronese, Bonifacio
see Pitati, de', Bonifacio

Veronese, Paolo
see Caliari, Paolo

Vicentino, Andrea
see Michieli, Andrea

Visentini, Antonio
Venice 1688-1782

308. *Perspective View*
Oil on canvas, 130 × 92 cm
(cat. n. 448)
Inscription: ANTONIO VISENTINI F., on parapet of balustrade on left
Acquisition: 1807, from the Old Academy of Venice
Last restored: 1859

Exhibited at the Ascension Day Fair of 1777, this picture is characteristic of the genre practised by Visentini, who was elected as an academician at the Institute's first enrolment on 13 February 1756. It denotes the importance of Pannini's ideas on the development of the artist, even though Visentini had by now accepted the neo-classical advance.

Bibliography: S.M.M., 1970, p. 120, n. 259.

Vivarini, Alvise

Murano, referred to as a minor in his mother's will of 1457 - d. between 1504 and 4 November 1505

309. *Madonna and Child enthroned between SS. Louis of Toulouse (or Bonaventura), Anthony of Padua, Anne, Joachim, Francis, and Bernardin of Siena*
Panel, 175 × 196 cm (cat. n. 607)
Inscription: ALVINE VIVA/RIN - P - MCCCCLXXX, on base of throne
Acquisition: 1812, following the suppression edicts
Last restored: 1979

The original place of this picture was over an altar dedicated to Santa Maria della Pra' and then to St. Bernardin in the Church of St. Francis at Treviso. The green awning, although extremely old, is a later addition and of matter impenetrable to radiography. In its first state the two windows overlooking the countryside at the back must have been wide open, as in the *Madonna adoring the sleeping Child* painted for the Venetian Church of San Giovanni in Bragora. As the most significant of Alvise's works, this picture reveals the artist as a sensitive interpreter of Antonello's example, which sought to construct a harmonious synthesis out of all the cultural elements contained in a painting. There is a study for the hands of the saints in the "Fondation de Custode" in Paris, while a half-length facsimile of St. Anthony is in the Correr Museum of Venice (see Correr Museum, p. 77, G. Romanelli, Electa, 1985: colour plate).

Bibliography: S.M.M., 1955, pp. 155-156; J. Steer, 1982, pp. 151-153.

310, 311. *St. John the Baptist, St. Matthew*
Panels, 134 × 52 cm and 133 × 51 cm (cat. ns. 618 and 619)
Acquisition: 1812, following the suppression edicts
Last restored: 1949

These panels, which are damaged at the top, were originally in the Church of St. Peter the Martyr in Murano. At their last restoration old repainting was removed and the Alvise authorship was re-established. It was also possible to give them a date immediately following the *Sacred Conversation* of 1480.
The cold, crystalline colouring, the sharply incisive brushwork, the space volumes and, at the saints' feet — particularly in the case of the Baptist — a bare and seemingly timeless countryside are characteristics which combine to place these figures among the most impressive of this artist's works.

Bibliography: S.M.M., 1955, pp. 154-155, nn. 172-173; J. Steer, 1982, pp. 150-151.

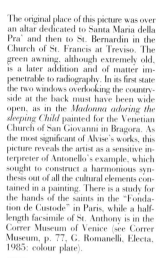

312, 313. *St. Clare, Martyr Saint*
Panels, 144 × 38 cm; 143 × 40 cm (cat. ns. 593, 593/a)
Acquisition: after becoming State property by Napoleonic decree the St. Clare panel was described in the catalogue of these Galleries for 1828; the *Martyr Saint* was sent to Vienna in 1838 and returned to the Galleries in 1919
Last restored: 1949 (*Martyr Saint*)

Noted by Boschini in 1664 in the Venetian Church of San Daniele. The austere, tormented face of St. Clare is depicted in such precise psychological terms that one almost feels this to be a real-life portrait. Outstanding amongst this artist's works of poetic and sensitive quality, the panel dates from between 1485 and 1490.

Bibliography: S.M.M., 1955, pp. 156-157, nn. 175-176; J. Steer, 1982, pp. 153-154.

Vivarini, Antonio
c. 1418/1420 - 1476/1484

314. *Madonna, with Child giving blessing*
Panel, gold background, 56 × 41 cm (cat. n. 1236)
Acquisition: 1959, from the Parish of San Giorgio delle Pertiche, where it had been placed on deposit in 1846
Last restored: 1958-1959

The original location of this devotional panel is not known, but its State provenance indicates that it once belonged to a public institution or body. This is further supported by a reference to judiciary assent written on the back of the picture in 1711 when it was taken for restoration. An extremely well unified work which, in spite of the gold background, appears to be seeking new volumetric qualities. The colour tones are tender and luminous suggesting the influence of Tuscan artists, notably of Masolino. The picture dates from c. 1440.

Bibliography: F. Valcanover, 1960, pp. 30-31; R. Pallucchini, 1962, pp. 16, 96.

315. *The Marriage of St. Monica*
Panel, gold background, 465 × 315 cm (cat. n. 50)
Inscription: QUI È COMO SANCTA MONIKA FU MANDATA A MARITO DAL PADRE E DA LA MADRE, at base
Acquisition: 1816, by legacy of Girolamo Molin. Exhibited in 1852 only, and from 1932 to 1951 stored in the Glass Museum at Murano
Last restored: 1951

Painting for the St. Monica altar in the Church of San Stefano where a wooden statue of this saint was once surrounded by "a series of historical episodes taken from her life" (Ridolfi, 1648). The small panels were dispersed in 1733 when the altar was dedicated to St. Stephen and

only four are known to have survived: the *Birth of St. Augustine* in the Courtauld Institute of Art, London, the *Baptism of St. Augustine* in the Carrara Academy, Bergamo, the *Conversion and Death of St. Monica's husband* in the Detroit Institute of Arts and *St. Monica in prayer* in a private Milanese collection. The signed work treated here draws on Masolino's colour tones, while revealing a new, if hesitant attempt in the perspective and spatial setting. The contemporary costumes recall those worn by Paolo Uccello's figures. The entire group must be of a slightly later date than 1441.

Bibliography: S.M.M., 1955, pp. 35-36; R. Pallucchini, 1962, pp. 26-27, 97.

Vivarini, Antonio
Giovanni D'Alemagna

316. *Triptych*
In central panel: *Madonna and Child enthroned, and angels*; in side panels: *SS. Gregory, Jerome, Ambrose and Augustine*
Three canvases: central, 344 × 203 cm; lateral, each 344 × 137 cm, with gilded stucco decoration (cat. n. 625)
Inscription: M - 4 - 46 - IOHANES - ALAMANUS/ANTONIUS - D - MURIANO, on plinth of throne
Acquisition: 1807, following the suppression edicts
Last restored: 1950

Originally in the Sala dell'Albergo of the Scuola della Carità where it adorned the wall facing Tiziano's *Presentation* (see n. 302), this triptych was once set in a carved wooden frame which was destroyed, together with its altar, when in 1811 Selva's plan to connect the various buildings with passages and steps was carried out. Among the oldest of surviving Venetian paintings on canvas, this

is undoubtedly the most significant piece of work in which the two artists. Vivarini and d'Alemagna are believed to have cooperated. The Virgin and angels, with their strong resemblance to Masolino's figures, are, however, almost certainly by the hand of Antonio Vivarini. The iconography is unusual for its "hortus conclusus" device circumscribing the *Sacred Conversation*.
The newly emerging sense of perspective is almost overpowered here by decorative effects which must have been even richer when the triptych was finished with its framework and stucco ornamentation, since vanished, on the copes of St. Augustine and St. Gregory. Contemporary with the beginning of Donatello's works at "the Santo", it is possible that the spatial definition of this painting may reflect a knowledge of that artist's early graphic studies in sculpture.

Bibliography: S.M.M., 1955, pp. 37-38, n. 36; R. Pallucchini, 1962, pp. 20-21, n. 104; G. Robertson, 1968, p. 6.

184

317. *Polyptych*
In central panel: *The Madonna enthroned and sleeping Child*; in side panels: *SS. Andrew, John the Baptist, Dominic and Peter*
Five panels, gold background: central 131 × 49 cm; lateral, each 107 × 33 cm (cat. n. 615)
Inscription: OPUS - BATOLOMEI VA RINI - DE MURANO - MCCCCLXIIII, on base of central panel
Acquisition: 1812, following the suppression edicts

Last restored: 1979

Formerly on the altar of the Ca' Morosini chapel (called "del Capitolo") in the Venetian Church of Sant'Andrea della Certosa. The old frame with a carved Crucifixion set between half-length figures of prophets along the top is lost, but a record remains in the engraving of G. Sasso. In some places the Virgin's cloak has been slightly spoiled.
In this picture the figurative vision of Mantegna is transformed by the painting

of the background in a bright variety of colours, while reminders of Gothic precedent are strongly marked in the contours. The result is one of the most expressive works of an artist who at other times was unable to free himself from an almost obsessive urge to make allusive play with his subject matter.

Bibliography: S.M.M., 1955, p. 159, n. 179; R. Pallucchini, 1962, pp. 38-39, 118.

318. *Polyptych*
In central panel: *St. Ambrose blessing devotees*; in side panels: *SS. Louis, Peter, Paul and Sebastian*
Five panels, gold background: central, 125 × 47 cm; lateral, each 108 × 36 cm (cat. n. 825)
Inscription: BARTHOLOMEUS VIVARINUS DE MURIANO PINXIT 1477, on base beneath St. Peter; IACOBUS DE FAENCIE IN CISIT, signature of frame-maker on base beneath St. Paul; S AMBR VIVIANI CAST SANT... VIC S PETRUS MUNTI SCRI E CONF..., dedicatory inscription beneath St. Ambrose written by the Steward of Art and brethren
Acquisition: 1919. Having become State property by the suppression decrees, the Polyptych was sent in

1838 to Vienna whence it was returned by restitutions made after the First World War
Last restored: 1979

There is some confusion as to the provenance of this work, the original frame carved by Giacomo da Faenza having been lost, as can be inferred from the inscription beneath St. Paul. It cannot be the altarpiece representing the stonemasons' craft, which in any case was later identified with a painting of Catena's, now in storage (cat. n. 988), but rather a devotional polyptych donated by a group of brethren and dedicated to their respective patron saints. The work has a surprisingly powerful quality of expression supported by a colour intensity of

equal strength. In spite of an accentuated plasticity, the stance of the figures against their gold background is one of iconic immobility, while the kneeling devotees are presented in the dwarfed form of medieval tradition.

Bibliography: S.M.M., 1955, pp. 159-160, n. 180; R. Pallucchini, 1962, pp. 48, 124.

319, 320. *St. Mary Madgalene, St. Barbara*
Panels, gold background, each 132×48 cm (cat. ns. 584, 585)

Inscription: BARTHOLOMEUS - VIVA - RINUS / DE MURANO - PINXIT - 1490, on a scroll beneath *St. Barbara*

Acquisition: 1812, following the suppression edicts

Last restored: 1979

These panels come from the destroyed Church of San Geminiano in Venice. Among the last works of Bartolomeo Vivarini's active life as an artist there is no doubt as to their authenticity and origin. They combine a formal nobility with a monumental look that comes almost as a harbinger of the 16th century.

Bibliography: S.M.M., 1955, pp. 160-161, nn. 181-182; R. Pallucchini, 1962, pp. 53, 130-131.

Vivarini, Bartolomeo
(and his workshop)

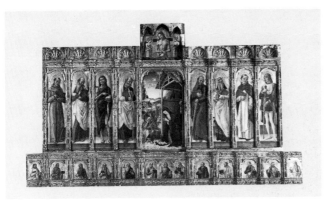

321. *Polyptych*
In central panel: *The Nativity*; in side panels, left: *SS. Francis, Andrew, John the Baptist, Peter*; right: *SS. Paul, Jerome, Dominic, Theodore*. In the cyma at top: *Christ between two angels*; in the predella at base: *Christ among the Apostles*. Known as the *Conversano Polyptych*
Panels, with gold background except the central one, 154×46 cm; lateral, each 138×23 cm; predella, 25×270 cm; cyma, 46×45 cm (cat. n. 581)

Inscription: HOC OPUS SUMPTIBUS DOMNI ANTHONII DE CHARITATE CA/NONICI ECCLESIE DE CONVERSANO IN FORMAM REDACTUM - EST - 1475, at foot of central panel; OPUS FACTUM VENETIIS PER BARTHOLOMEUM VIVARINUM..., on listel at centre of the predella frame

Acquisition: 1883, by purchase from the Cathedral of Conversano

Last restored: 1948

Painted in 1475 for the Cathedral of Conversano at the expense of its clergy, as stated in the inscription beneath the central panel. Destined for a remote town near Bari in southern Italy, the work must have placed less binding obligations on the artist than was normally the case. In fact, if the central group is in stronger plastic relief than in Antonio Vivarini's painting of 1447, now in Prague, the saints in the lateral panels and the predella are of weaker execution and appear to be by different hands.

Bibliography: S.M.M., 1955, pp. 161-162, n. 183; R. Pallucchini, 1962, pp. 47, 122.

Vivarini, Bartolomeo
(his circle)

322. *Polyptych*
Central panel: *The Madonna enthroned and Child*; side panels, left: *SS. Thomas and Vincent*; right: *Peter the Martyr and Anthony the Abbot*
Three panels, gold background: central, 46 × 25 cm; lateral, each 46 × 31 cm (cat. n. 27)
Inscription: B. VIVARINI, fictitious signature on central panel
Acquisition: 1816, by legacy of Girolamo Molin
Last restored: 1979

In a mediocre state of conservation, these panels have been attributed also to Quirizio da Murano and to Bastiani.

Bibliography: S.M.M., 1955, p. 162.

Zais, Giuseppe
Forno di Canale di Agordo 1709 - Treviso 1781

323. *Ruins of a vaulted building*
Oil on canvas, 97 × 147 cm (cat. n. 846)
Acquisition: 1923, from the Royal Palace, Venice
Last restored: 1984

It is certain that this landscape and the next one were painted at the end of the 1730s. The influence of Marco Ricci's example on the growth of Zais' talent is clearly evident, even though the former treated the changing aspects of light and atmosphere perhaps with more fluency and style when painting the landscape of the Agordino.

Bibliography: S.M.M., 1970, p. 121, n. 260.

324. *Ancient ruins with large archway and columns*
Oil on canvas, 89 × 147 cm (cat. n. 847)
Acquisition: 1923, from the Royal Palace, Venice

This picture reminds us, like the previous one, of a similar vein of inventiveness in the later works of Marco Ricci.

Bibliography: S.M.M., 1970, p. 121, n. 261.

325. *Landscape with rushing torrent and country-folk dancing*
Oil on canvas, 98 × 143 cm (cat. n. 848)
Acquisition: 1923, from the Royal Palace, Venice
Last restored: 1984

A companion picture to the next one sharing, in both instances, Zais' commitment to introducing a more pleasing harmony of colour and more attractive subjects into the teaching of Marco Ricci and the example of Zuccarelli.
Bibliography: S.M.M., 1970, p. 121, n. 262.

326. *Landscape with river, bridge and herded flock*
Oil on canvas, 97 × 143 cm (cat. n. 849)
Acquisition: 1923, from the Royal Palace, Venice
Last restored: 1938

Here the subject is typical of those chosen by Zuccarelli, but the springlike, Arcadian freshness of the Tuscan artist's settings is applied at a level corresponding more closely with real life, and with decorative rustic simplicity.

Bibliography: S.M.M., 1970, p. 122, n. 263.

327. *The Swing*
Oil on canvas, 55 × 39 cm
(cat. n. 1309)
Acquisition: 1957, from the Royal
Palace, Venice
Last restored: 1957

This small canvas and the three that
follow, all of them the work of Zais'
mature years, demonstrate the interest
that the artist showed in contemporary
French painting. Thus in *The Swing* we
note that he has brought rustic charm to
some of the motifs of Watteau's *Fête
champêtre* now in the Edinburgh Art
Gallery. Zais knew that picture from the
engraving of it made in 1732 by Laurent
Cars.

Bibliography: S.M.M., 1970, p. 123, n.
267.

328. *An open-air concert*
Oil on canvas, 55 × 39 cm
(cat. n. 1310)
Acquisition: 1957, from the Royal
Palace, Venice
Last restored: 1957

The group of figures central to this delightful composition *à la française* is copied
from the small painting of a *Young
Woman and four masqueraders of the
Commedia dell'arte* which can be seen
in the National Museum of Stockholm.
The artist knew it from an engraving of
the picture by G. Scotin.

Bibliography: S.M.M., 1970, p. 123, n.
268.

329. *Pierrot with couples*
Oil on canvas, 55 × 39 cm
(cat. n. 1311)
Acquisition: 1957, from the Royal
Palace, Venice
Last restored: 1957

This work in which Pierrot makes himself
a centre of interest to the couples derives
very clearly both in spirit and form from
French "galante" painting of the day.

Bibliography: S.M.M., 1970, p. 123, n.
269.

330. *Couples near a fountain*
Oil on canvas, 55 × 39 cm
(cat. n. 1312)
Acquisition: 1957, from the Royal
Palace, Venice
Last restored: 1957

This series of four rustic scenes ends with
a gallant meeting near a fountain.
Together, these pictures illustrate the
close relations between Venice and Paris,
the two main centres of art during the
first half of the 18th century.

Bibliography: S.M.M., 1970, p. 123, n.
270.

331. *Landscape with fountain*
Oil on canvas, 132 × 80 cm
(cat. n. 447)

Inscription: G.Z.F., the initials of the
artist at lower left

Acquisition: 1807, from the Old
Academy of Venice

Last restored: 1962

It was with this painting that Zais applied
for election to the Academy in 1765. His
request was not granted until 11 September 1774.

Bibliography: S.M.M., 1970, p. 122, n.
266.

Zais, Giuseppe
(attributed to)

332. *Landscape with Agar and the angel*
Oil on canvas, 72 × 96 cm
(cat. n. 721)

Acquisition: 1906, by purchase from
Maria Campostella of Treviso

Last restored: 1984

In some respects this landscape and the
next display characteristics which are
much nearer to the style of Antonio Diziani than to that of Zais.

Bibliography: S.M.M., 1970, p. 122, n.
264.

333. *Landscape with Tobias
(Tobiolo) and the angel*
Oil on canvas, 71 × 95 cm
(cat. n. 722)

Acquisition: 1906, by purchase from
Maria Campostella of Treviso

Last restored: 1984

As with the painting described above, in
this landscape the impasto lacks the usual
substantial quality and thickness generally associated with Zais.

Bibliography: S.M.M., 1970, p. 122, n.
265.

Zoppo, Marco (?)
see Marco Antonio di Ruggero (?)

Zotti, Gianfrancesco
(Gianfrancesco da Tolmezzo)
c. 1450 - records until 1510

334. *Madonna and Child, angels
playing music*
Panel, 82 × 54 cm (cat. n. 723)
Inscription: ZUANE FRANCE(SC)O
DE/TOLMEZZO, on left side at base
Acquisition: 1906, by gift of Antonio
Dal Zotto
Last restored: 1979

This is the same picture that Cavalcaselle
noted in 1876 as belonging to avv. Astori
in Udine. Along with a rather ingenuous
interpretation of Mantegna's style the artist brings to this painting a new element
of form and composition which implies
an attempt to develop further the example of the Bellinis and of Antonello (da
Messina). The typology of the singing
angels, who resemble those around the
Provesano *Crucifixion*, suggests a date
between 1495 and 1498.

Bibliography: S.M.M., 1955, pp.
129-130, n. 132; A. Rizzi, 1978, p. 288.

Zuccarelli, Francesco
Pitigliano 1702 - Florence 1788/1789

335. *Chasing the bull*
Oil on canvas, 114 × 150 cm
(cat. n. 864)
Acquisition: 1949, from the Royal
Palace, Venice
Last restored: 1984

Originally in the Benedictine Monastery
of San Giorgio Maggiore, there is good
reason to suppose that this is one of Zuccarelli's early works and that it was
painted soon after 1732. In that year he
settled in Venice having painted land-
scapes in the Tuscan workshop of Paolo
Anesi and gained experience in figure
design in Rome by studies based on the
drawings of Morandi and Pietro Nelli. But
it was the landscape of Marco Ricci and
Zais that influenced Zuccarelli more than
anything in his predilection for idealised,
arcadian painting, as in his *Chasing the
bull*. He was much sought after in artistic
circles in Paris, and in London where he
spent many years and was to become one
of George III's favourite painters.

Bibliography: S.M.M., 1970, p. 125.

336. *The Adbuction of Europa*
Oil on canvas, 142 × 208 cm
(cat. n. 858)
Inscription: ZUCARELI, on collar of dog
at lower left
Acquisition: 1923, from the Royal
Palace, Venice
Last restored: 1982

This and several of the canvases that
follow were painted for the Pisani family who kept them until the end of the
18th century in their splendid villa at
Stra, near Venice. The scene of the abduction of Europa (see Homer's *Iliad*)
is set in the rhythms of a minuet in the
idyllic surroundings of a landscape of
green meadows and pale blue waters.

Bibliography: S.M.M., 1970, p. 126, n.
287.

337. *Bacchanal*
Oil on canvas, 142 × 208 cm
(cat. n. 859)
Acquisition: 1923, from the Royal
Palace, Venice
Last restored: 1982

In a setting of idealised rural serenity,
with a classical temple peeping through
the rose-coloured mists on the right, we
see fauns and maidens dancing together,
their limbs forming an arabesque pattern
ignored by drowsy Bacchus who dozes
on the left in the shade of a rustic shanty.

Bibliography: S.M.M., 1970, p. 126, n.
288.

338. *Landscape with hunter resting*
Oil on canvas, 78 × 98 cm
(cat. n. 1333)
Acquisition: 1959, from the Royal Palace, Venice
Last restored: 1959

Believed to have been painted for the Monastery of San Giorgio Maggiore, this landscape of the 1740s does not conform with the artist's usual concept of Nature filtered through the blissful calm of the Arcadian dreams of his day. Grouped around the resting hunter are his horse and two dogs, realistic, charming in their natural way, a sign that Zuccarelli was well acquainted with the Dutch landscape artists such as Berchem and Wouwermann.

Bibliography: S.M.M., 1970, p. 125, n. 286.

339. *Landscape with young persons beside a stream*
Oil on canvas, 118 × 137 cm
(cat. n. 860)
Acquisition: 1923, from the Royal Palace, Venice
Last restored: 1984

This landscape and the two immediately following, together with a fourth (cat. n. 863) now on deposit at Ca' Rezzonico, at one time belonged to the Pisani family. They all date from the very early 1750s. With exceptional skill Zuccarelli sets out a rustic scene with gentle youth charmingly posed in the foreground against the burgeoning green of Spring. Step by step the landscape, shown in all its detail, recedes towards a distant horizon which is immersed in golden mist.

Bibliography: S.M.M., 1970, p. 127.

340. *Landscape with woman on horseback*
Oil on canvas, 118 × 136 cm
(cat. n. 861)
Acquisition: 1923, from the Royal Palace, Venice
Last restored: 1984

No less well considered than in the picture above is the setting chosen for this pastoral scene. It may be noted that the group, depicted with a feathery yet precise touch, is so placed as to stand out against a steep hill which on its right reveals the way to the half-hidden countryside and the vaporous sweetness of its water and trees.

Bibliography: S.M.M., 1970, p. 127, n. 290.

341. *Landscape with boy fishing*
Oil on canvas, 118 × 136 cm
(cat. n. 862)
Acquisition: 1923, from the Royal Palace, Venice
Last restored: now in course

Again in this landscape, cleverly caught in a wide embrace of open sky, man and nature are depicted in detail with a light and cheerful pictorial freshness.

Bibliography: S.M.M., 1970, p. 127, n. 291.

342. *Landscape with John the Baptist*
Oil on canvas, 132 × 94 cm
(cat. n. 458)
Acquisition: 1807, from the Old Academy of Venice
Last restored: 1960

This is the picture that Zuccarelli painted when applying for election to the Venice Academy on 16 February 1763. The cold anonymity of John the Baptist is in marked contrast with the happy inclusion of a vividly pictorial background to a dramatic landscape.

Bibliography: S.M.M., 1970, p. 128, n. 293.

Bibliography

B. Aikema, "Pietro della Vecchia - A Profile", in *Saggi e memorie di storia dell'arte*, 13, 1982.

P. Askev, "The Parabole Painting of Domenico Fetti", in *The Art Bulletin*, 1961.

M. Azzi Visentini, "Antonio Badile", in *Maestri della pittura veronese*, Verona 1974.

A. Ballarin, "Una nuova prospettiva su Giorgione: la ritrattistica degli anni 1500-1503", in *Giorgione - Convegno internazionale di studi*, Castelfranco Veneto 1978.

N. Barcham, "Giambattista Tiepolo's Ceiling for S. Maria di Nazareth in Venice: Legend, Traditions and Devotions", in *The Art Bulletin*, 61, 1979.

J.G. Bernasconi, "The Dating of the Cycle of the Miracles of the Cross from the Scuola di San Giovanni Evangelista", in *Arte Veneta*, XXXV, 1981.

G. Bissali, "L'Apocalisse nell'opera pittorica di Jacobello Alberegno", in *Liber Annus*, XXX (1980), Studium Biblicum Franciscanum P.O. Box 19424. Jerusalem.

S. Borla, "Paolo Veneziano e il fratello Marco", in *Arte Veneta*, XXIV (1970), pp. 199-204.

A. Bosero, *L'opera completa del Crivelli*, Milano 1975.

M. Boskovits, "Ferrarese Painting about 1450: Some New Arguments", in *Burlington Magazine*, 903, CXX, 1978.

E. Camesasca, *L'opera completa del Bellotto*, Milano 1974.

C. Cierivia, "Allegorie morali dalla bottega belliniana", in *Giorgione e la cultura veneta tra '400 e '500*, Roma 1981.

C. Ciolino, "Antonello de Saliba", in *Antonello da Messina*, exhibition cat., Roma 1981.

R. Cocke, in *The Genius of Venice 1500-1600*, exhibition cat., London 1983.

M. Colusso, *La Scuola Grande di S. Teodoro*, Venezia 1981.

A. Conti, *Storia del restauro*, Milano.

P.J. Cooney - G. Malfarina, *L'opera completa di Annibale Carracci*, Milano 1976.

L. Cuppini, "Niccolò di Pietro: l'arrivo dei Magi", in *Arte Veneta*, XVIII, 1964.

G. Dalla Vestra - D. De Paoli Benedetti, *I pittori bellunesi prima del Vecellio*, Verona 1975.

J. Daniels, *Sebastiano Ricci*, Hove (Sussex) 1976.

F. D'Arcais, "Le tavole con le storie di S. Benedetto: un problema ancora aperto", in *Arte Veneta*, XXX, 1976.

B. Degenhart - A. Schmitt, *Corpus der italienischen Zeichnungen 1300-1450, Teil II, Venedig*, Berlin 1980.

A. De Nicolò Salmazo, "Un libro su Alvise Vivarini", in *Arte Veneta*, XXXVII, 1983.

P. De Vecchi, *L'opera completa di Piero della Francesca*, Milano 1967.

G.T. Faggin, "Bonifacio ai Camerlenghi", in *Arte Veneta*, 1963.

G.T. Faggin, *L'opera completa di Memling*, Milano 1969.

C. Furlan, *Il Pordenone*, exhibition cat., Milano 1984.

G. Gamulin, "Ritornando sul Quattrocento", in *Arte Veneta*, XVII, 1963.

G. Gamulin, "Contributi alla pittura del Quattrocento", in *Arte Veneta*, XXXVII, 1983.

N. Garavaglia, *L'opera completa del Mantegna*, Milano 1967.

G. Gatto, "Per la cronologia di Rosalba Carriera", in *Arte Veneta*, 1971.

D. Gioseffi, "Giorgione e la pittura tonale", in *Giorgione - Convegno internazionale di studi*, Castelfranco Veneto 1978.

M. Hirst, *Sebastiano del Piombo*, Oxford 1981.

P. Humfrey, *Cima da Conegliano*, Cambridge 1983.

C. Huter, "The Ceneda Master", in *Arte Veneta*, XXVII, 1973.

C. Huter, "Jacobello del Fiore, Giambono and the St. Benedict Panels", in *Arte Veneta*, XXXII, 1978.

Il restauro del Convito in casa di Levi di Paolo Veronese, n. 11, Venezia 1984.

Johann Liss, exhibition cat., Augsburg 1975.

S. Kozakiewicz, *Bernardo Bellotto*, Milano 1972.

R. Longhi, "Ritorni e progressi su Alvise", in *Paragone*, 229, 1969.

M. Lucco, in *Proposte di restauro: dipinti del primo Cinquecento nel Veneto*, exhibition cat., Castelfranco Veneto 1978.

M. Lucco, *Sebastiano del Piombo*, Milano 1980.

192   L. Magagnato, *Da Altichiero a Pisanello*, exhibition cat., Venezia 1958.

L. Magagnato, in *Da Tiziano a El Greco*, exhibition cat., Venezia 1981.

G. Mandel, *L'opera completa di Antonello da Messina*, Milano 1967.

G. Mariacher, "Scultori caronesi e comaschi a Venezia", in *Arte e artisti dei laghi lombardi - I. Architetti e scultori del Quattrocento*, Como 1959.

G. Mariacher, "Jacopo Negretti detto Palma il Vecchio", in *I pittori bergamaschi dal XIII al XIX secolo*, I, Bergamo 1975.

G. Mariani Canova, *L'opera completa del Lotto* (preface by R. Pallucchini), Milano 1975.

G. Mariani Canova, in *Da Tiziano a El Greco*, exhibition cat., Venezia 1981.

G. Mariani Canova, in *Paris Bordon*, Milano 1984.

R. Mariuz, *L'opera completa del Piazzetta* (preface by R. Pallucchini), Milano 1982.

E. Martini, *La pittura del Settecento veneto*, Udine 1983.

S. Mason Rinaldi, "Contributi d'archivio per la decorazione pittorica della Scuola di San Giovanni Evangelista", in *Arte Veneta*, XXXII, 1978.

S. Mason Rinaldi, *Palma il Giovane*, Milano 1984.

L. Menegazzi, *Cima da Conegliano*, Treviso 1981.

E. Merkel, in *Giorgione a Venezia*, exhibition cat., Milano 1978.

J. Meyer zur Capellen, *La "figura" del San Lorenzo Giustiniani di Jacopo Bellini*, Venezia 1981 (Centro Tedesco di Studi Veneziani, *Quaderni*, n. 19).

R. Molajoli, *L'opera completa di Cosmè Tura e i grandi pittori ferraresi del suo tempo*, Milano 1974.

A. Morassi, *Guardi*, Venezia 1973.

L. Moretti, in *Venezia e Bisanzio*, exhibition cat., Venezia 1974.

L. Mortari, *Bernardo Strozzi*, Roma 1966.

V. Moschini, "Altri restauri alle Gallerie di Venezia", in *Bollettino d'Arte*, XLV, 1960.

S. Moschini Marconi, *Gallerie dell'Accademia di Venezia - Opere d'arte dei secoli XIV e XV*, Roma 1955.

S. Moschini Marconi, *Gallerie dell'Accademia di Venezia - Opere d'arte del secolo XVI*, Roma 1962.

S. Moschini Marconi, *Gallerie dell'Accademia di Venezia - Opere d'arte dei secoli XVII, XVIII, XIX*, Roma 1970.

S. Moschini Marconi, in *Giorgione a Venezia*, exhibition cat., Milano 1978.

T. Mullay, "Two Modelli by Andrea Vicentino", in *The Burlington Magazine*, CVI, 1964.

M. Muraro, *Paolo da Venezia*, Milano 1969.

M. Muraro, "La pittura devozionale e la diffusione dello squarcionismo", in *Ateneo Veneto*, 1975.

G. Nepi Sciré, "Appunti e chiarimenti su Gerolamo da Treviso il Vecchio (Gerolamo Aviano o Gerolamo Pennacchi?)", in *Notizie da Palazzo Albani*, II, n. 3, 1973.

G. Nepi Sciré, "Andrea da Murano", in *Venezia e la peste*, exhibition cat., Venezia 1979.

G. Nepi Sciré, "Il pittore trevigiano Pier Maria Pennacchi", in *Lorenzo Lotto - Convegno internazionale di studi*, Venezia 1980.

G. Nepi Sciré, "Pier Maria Pennacchi: regesti, documenti e proposte", in *Bollettino d'Arte*, 6, 1980.

G. Nepi Sciré, "Il restauro della Presentazione al Tempio di Tiziano", in *Bollettino d'Arte*, 5, Roma 1984.

G. Nepi Sciré, *Recenti restauri alle Gallerie dell'Accademia*, Venezia 1985.

R. Pallucchini, "Nuove proposte per Niccolò di Pietro", in *Arte Veneta*, X, 1956.

R. Pallucchini, *La pittura veneta del Quattrocento*, Padova 1958-1959.

R. Pallucchini, "Pantaleon pinsit", in *Arte Veneta*, XIII-XIV, 1959-1960.

R. Pallucchini, *Pittura veneziana del Settecento*, Milano 1960.

R. Pallucchini, *I Vivarini*, Venezia 1962.

R. Pallucchini, *La pittura veneziana del Trecento*, Roma 1964.

R. Pallucchini, *Tiziano*, Milano 1969.

R. Pallucchini, in *Venezia e Bisanzio*, exhibition cat., Venezia 1974.

R. Pallucchini, *La pittura veneziana del Seicento*, I, Milano 1981.

R. Pallucchini, *Bassano*, Bologna 1982.

R. Pallucchini, *Veronese*, Milano 1984.

R. Pallucchini - P. Rossi, *Tintoretto - Le opere sacre e profane*, Milano 1982.

R. Pallucchini - F. Rossi, *Cariani*, Bergamo 1983.

G. Panazza, *Mostra di Girolamo Romanino*, Brescia 1965.

A. Paolucci, "Benedetto Diana", in *Paragone*, XVII, n. 199/19, 1966.

A. Parronchi, "Passaggio della prospettiva da Firenze a Venezia", in *Giorgione - Convegno internazionale di studi*, Castelfranco Veneto 1978.

G. Pavanello, *L'opera completa del Canova*, Milano 1976.

F. Pedrocco, "Scuola di Sant'Orsola", in *Le Scuole di Venezia*, ed. by T. Pignatti, Milano 1981.

T. Pignatti, *Pietro Longhi*, Venezia 1968.

T. Pignatti, *L'opera completa di Giovanni Bellini detto Giambellino*, Milano 1969.

T. Pignatti, *Giorgione*, Venezia 1969 and 1978.

T. Pignatti, *Paolo Veronese*, Venezia 1976.

L. Puppi, *Bartolomeo Montagna*, Venezia 1962.

L. Puppi, in *Dopo Mantegna - Arte a Padova e nel territorio nei secoli XV e XVI*, Milano 1976.

L. Puppi, "Riflessioni su tempi e problemi della ritrattistica del Lotto", in *Lorenzo Lotto - Convegno internazionale di studi*, Venezia 1980.

C.L. Ragghianti, "Ricerche e attribuzioni", in *Critica d'Arte*, XLII, 1977, pp. 151-153.

F.L. Richardson, *Andrea Schiavone*, Oxford 1980.

Riflettoscopia computerizzata infrarosso, 6, Venezia 1984.

A. Rizzi, in *Friuli Venezia Giulia*, Milano 1978.

G. Robertson, *Giovanni Bellini*, Oxford 1968.

P. Rossi, *Jacopo Tintoretto - I ritratti*, Venezia 1973.

M. Rothlisberger, "Studi su Jacopo Bellini", in *Saggi e memorie di storia dell'arte*, Venezia 1959.

A. Ruggeri, "Giovanni Bellini, Vanitas", in *Giorgione a Venezia*, exhibition cat., Milano 1978.

A. Ruggeri, "Giovanni Bellini - La Pietà", in *Giorgione a Venezia*, exhibition cat., Milano 1978.

U. Ruggeri, in *Giambattista Piazzetta e la sua scuola*, exhibition cat., Venezia 1983.

Ph. Rylands, "Palma il Vecchio Assumption of the Virgin", in *Burlington Magazine*, 119, 1977.

B. Sani, "Alcune precisazioni sugli autoritratti di Rosalba Carriera", in *Per Maria Cionini Visani - Scritti di amici*, 1977.

Marin Sanudo il Giovane, *De origine, situ et magistratibus urbis Venetae ovvero la Città di Venezia (1493-1530)*, ed. by A. Caracciolo Aricò, Milano 1980.

A. Scarpa Sonino, "Per un catalogo di Niccolò di Pietro", in *Atti dell'Istituto Veneto di Scienze Lettere ed Arti*, CXXXIV, 1975-1976.

J. Schulz, *Venetian Painted Ceilings of the Renaissance*, Berkeley and Los Angeles, 1968.

G. Schweikhart, "Giorgione e Bellini", in *Giorgione e l'Umanesimo veneziano*, Firenze 1981.

V. Sgarbi, *Carpaccio*, Bologna 1979.

S. Simonetti, in *The Genius of Venice 1500-1600*, exhibition cat., London 1983.

S. Sinding - Larsen, *Christ in the Council Hall Studies in the Religious Iconography of Venetian Republic*, Institutum Romanum Norvegiae Acta ad Archaeologiam et Artium Historiam Pertinentia, V, Roma 1974.

I. Steer, *Alvise Vivarini - His Art and Influence*, Cambridge 1982.

J. Stock, *Disegni veneti di collezioni inglesi*, exhibition cat., Vicenza 1980.

F. Valcanover, "Aggiunta al catalogo di Antonio Vivarini", in *Paragone*, 123, 1960.

F. Valcanover, "New Light on Alessandro Longhi's Balotin del Doxe", in *The Connoisseur*, 1961.

F. Valcanover, *Restauri nel Veneto 1965*, I, Venezia 1966.

F. Valcanover, in *Da Tiziano a El Greco*, exhibition cat., Venezia 1981.

F. Valcanover, "Gli Eremiti di Giovanni Girolamo Savoldo delle Gallerie dell'Accademia", in *Atti del convegno su Girolamo Savoldo*, Brescia 1984.

L. Vertova, "Bernardino Licinio", in *I pittori bergamaschi dal XIII al XIX secolo - Il Cinquecento*, I, Bergamo 1975.

H.E. Wethey, *The Paintings of Titian: I. The Religious Paintings*, London 1969.

E. Young, "Michele Marieschi, Another Signed View of Venice and His Capricci of Palace or Prison Interiors?", in *The Connoisseur*, September 1977.

P. Zampetti, *Lorenzo Lotto*, Bologna 1983.

P. Zampetti - J. Chiappini, "Andrea Previtali", in *I pittori bergamaschi dal XIII al XIX secolo - Il Cinquecento*, I, Bergamo 1975.

194   F. Zava Boccazzi, *Pittoni*, Venezia 1979.

F. Zeri, "Qualcosa su Nicola di Maestro Antonio",
in *Paragone*, 107, 1958.

A.P. Zugni Tauro, *Gaspare Diziani*, Milano 1971.

F. Zuliani, in *Venezia e Bisanzio*, exhibition cat.,
Venezia 1974 (n. 76).

Legend

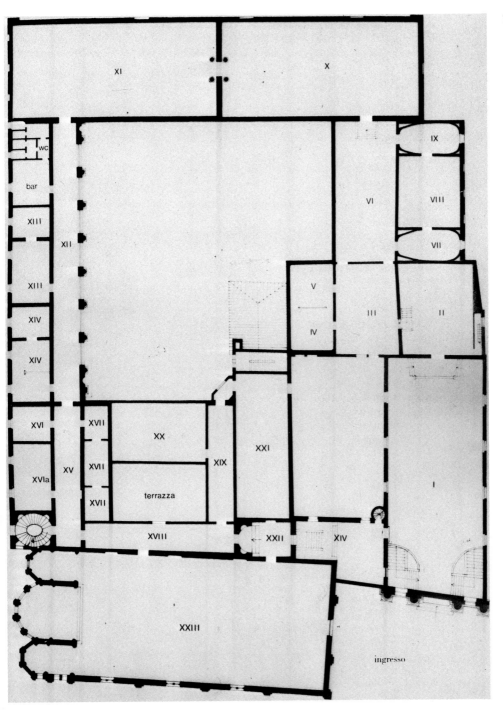

Photographic Credits
Sergio Anelli, Electa
Foto Fiorentini, Venezia
Foto Rossi, Venezia
Antonio Guerra, Bologna
Soprintendenza per i
Beni Artistici e Storici,
Venezia

Printed on behalf of
Edizioni Electa SpA - Milan
by Fantonigrafica. Venice